The uniting of Europe

The Making of the Contemporary World

Edited by Eric Evans and Ruth Henig University of Lancaster

The Making of the Contemporary World series provides challenging interpretations of contemporary issues and debates within strongly defined historical frameworks. The range of the series is global, with each volume drawing together material from a range of disciplines – including economics, politics and sociology. The books in this series present compact, indispensable introductions for students studying the modern world.

Forthcoming titles include:

Thatcher and Thatcherism
Eric J Evans
The Soviet Union in World Politics, 1945–1991
Geoffrey Roberts
The Uniting of Europe
From Discord to Concord
Stanley Henig
International Economy since 1945
Sidney Pollard
The United Nations in the Contemporary World
David Whittaker
Latin America
John Ward
China Under Communism
Alan Lawrance
The Cold War
An Interdisciplinary History
David Painter
The Green Movement
Dick Richardson
The Irish Question
Patrick Maume
Decolonization
Raymond Betts
Right Wing Extremism
Paul Hainsworth

The uniting of Europe

From discord to concord

Stanley Henig

London and New York

First published 1997
by Routledge
11 New Fetter Lane, London EC4P 4EE

Simultaneously published in the USA and Canada
by Routledge
29 West 35th Street, New York, NY 10001

Typeset in Times by Routledge
Printed and bound in Great Britain by
Clays Ltd, St. Ives PLC

British Library Cataloguing in Publication Data
A catalogue record for this book is available from the British Library

Library of Congress Cataloguing in Publication Data
A catalogue record has been requested

ISBN 0–415–13693–8

Contents

Introduction

This book has a multiple focus. First it offers an account of the development of European integration, starting in Chapter 1 with an analysis of the problems confronting Europe in 1945 and continuing after the Maastricht Treaty on European Union through to current discussions amongst member governments of that Union as to future progress. Second, it seeks to explain the progress of integration by placing it in the wider context of world politics and economics. A central thesis of the book is that the process of integration has throughout been conditioned by, and can only be explained by reference to, that wider context. Two features of that context have been pre-eminent – the need to find a solution to what might be termed the 'German' problem and from 1945 at least to 1989 the division of Europe into East and West, which resulted from past failures to solve that problem. Third, the book looks at the very special case of the United Kingdom, seeking to explain apparent alternations in policy – initial unwillingness to join the European Community, followed by protracted negotiations for membership and then the lengthy period as an apparently reluctant European. Finally, particularly in Chapters 4 and 8, there are analyses of the ways in which the Community, now renamed the European Union, actually operates in practice, with attention being given to the various foundation treaties and the structure and function of the major institutions.

This short work cannot aspire to offer any grand theory as to the relative roles of historic inevitability and human choice in determining the course of events. However, the entire analysis contained within this book is deeply influenced by two considerations. The first is that the arguments for integration are not really founded on idealism, but rather on a particular and hard-headed view of the problems confronting the continent and the best ways of solving them. The founders of what may become a united Europe differ from their critics not because they are and have been idealists, but rather because they have adopted a programme for defining Europe's future which is in tune with current realities. The second is a recognition that there are certain key moments in history which are sometimes termed as watersheds or turning points. My own preferred phrase is 'defining moments'. It is an elusive concept, but my central argument is that preceding events have built up to the moment when a key decision has to be taken. There is no need to reinvoke the argument between choice and inevitability. The direction taken from a defining moment determines events until the next defining moment. One such was the British decision in 1939 to go to war with Nazi Germany before rather than after the latter conquered most of the continent. However inevitable the decision, it was a matter of choice which powerfully conditioned subsequent events until 1945, when what was left of the continent reached another watershed.

1   Europe in 1945

The Second World War consolidated the verdict of the First in shifting irrevocably the balance of world power away from Europe. Two phases summarise the purely military conflict in Europe. In the First, Germany conquered almost the entire continent. In the Second, two essentially extraneous forces – the USA and the USSR – defeated Germany and liberated Europe. The USA with its British and other allies, on the one hand, and the Soviet Union, on the other, fought substantially separate campaigns against German armies. There were no joint operations and no joint military command. With Germany defeated, the victorious armies simply occupied adjoining space. Thus Western Europe was liberated by US-led forces and Eastern and Central by the Red Army. It is possible to attribute the later division of Europe to agreements made by Churchill, Roosevelt and Stalin at Yalta and elsewhere. The reality is that these agreements were determined to all intents and purposes by the military situation on the ground whilst Germany was being defeated. The so-called Iron Curtain which descended in the middle of Europe was brought about by the realities of power and not by any treaties. Indeed even now, fifty years later, there has been no attempt to emulate 1919 with a comprehensive series of peace treaties. In the immediate aftermath of 1945 the settlement was purely military; and ironically it was to last very much longer.

Extending this Euro-centric approach, it is worth considering also the impact on European states of the world-wide conflict. At a simplistic level the war beyond Europe was equally a struggle against aggression and the final defeat of Japan was as decisive as that of Germany. However, for those imperial European countries involved outside their own continent, the flow of the war and the issues involved were in many ways more complex whilst the final verdict was not so clear cut. To all intents and purposes, the European states lost effective control of their overseas territories partly as a result of their own internal collapse, partly from defeat by the Japanese and partly from the new world order and very different imperialisms favoured by the new super-powers. Prior to 1939 there was a significant interlink between the domestic economies of Britain, France, Belgium, the Netherlands and Portugal and their overseas 'possessions'. The loss of the link could not fail to affect these same European economies. There is a difference in reactions to the verdicts of the internal and external conflicts. No European politician or leader could fail to recognise the military verdict of the European war and its stark political implications. There are quite different dimensions to assessment of this external conflict. The purely military verdict concealed political realities and their economic implications.

Militarily Europe was dependent on its liberators and potentially at their mercy. Disagreements between those liberators were another ingredient in a dangerous world. However, in another sense Europe had also lost its political paramountcy. The system of predominantly nation states as established by the 1919 settlement had simply collapsed. With the exceptions of Britain, Sweden and Switzerland, every European state had witnessed either the relatively violent overthrow of its constitutional arrangements or had been militarily occupied by an enemy or both. There had always been some ethical dimensions to imperialism. European countries could claim prior to 1939 to be offering something by way of 'political tutelage' to their colonies. Political collapse and military defeats in Europe and elsewhere destroyed such illusions. Confronted with former imperial possessions looking for their own independence, Europe lacked both the physical means and the moral authority to make any effective response. Resistance to the reality that the old colonial empires had gone for ever was to store up considerable potential for de-stabilising domestic politics.

The collapse of so many nation states in the period 1920–45 is particularly significant in the evolution of ideas for uniting Europe. Throughout the nineteenth century, the nation state had been presented as the legitimate alternative to the old hybrid monarchies and empires which dominated much of Europe. It was easy to assume that there was a natural alliance between nationalism and liberalism as the two new 'dynamic' forces. Nationalism was posited as creative and liberating: few appreciated its destructive potential. By 1914 significant numbers of national groups had won the right to have their 'own' state.

Whatever its shortcomings as a settlement, Versailles legitimated these and other claims. As a result, more peoples than at any time in Europe's previous history could boast of their 'own' state. Adoption of liberal democratic systems by these new states seemed to confirm the nineteenth-century view that nationalism was creative and basically benevolent. A short excursion into the politics of many of the states of Central and Eastern Europe quickly belies the myth. It is a common-place assertion that the united Germany of Bismarck was begotten in violence. It is all too often forgotten that the post-1919 successor states were themselves established as a result of a very much bloodier conflict than any provoked by Bismarck. In most cases few of the conditions for liberal democracy were present. This was soon reflected in the turbulent politics and frequent resorts to violence which characterised so many of these new states.[1]

In Central and Eastern Europe the verdict of 1939–45 removed any element of choice about future forms of political organisation. Regimes and governments would have to be acceptable to the USSR. The Communists simply swallowed or outlawed other political forces. However, nationalism in effect went underground – to emerge two generations later as, in most cases, the one legitimate alternative to the regime.

Western Europe was different. The history of nation states was longer, and in most cases there had been a gradual evolution of polit-ical structures. Prior to 1939 Germany, Italy and Portugal adopted fascist regimes, as did Spain after a civil war the outcome of which was decided by foreign intervention. Other states in Western Europe survived internal dissension. Although fascist and neo-fascist parties appeared throughout Europe, parliamentary democracy was in no real danger elsewhere in the Western part of the continent. However, most countries fell to military aggression in the early part of the war and this led to the imposition of new regimes which sometimes included these same native fascist groups. Throughout the whole of Europe, the price of military defeat was without precedent. It led to occupation and subordination of the entire machinery of government to the victors for whom the spoils of war were unlimited. It is traditional for defeated armies to surrender, but now this extended to the entire citi-zenry. It is this more than anything else which gives the phrase 'total war' its resonance.

These shared formative experiences are crucial to an understanding of post-war developments. The philosophical basis for organised society is that the individual is protected against external aggression and given a framework of law and order within which to carry on with daily life. Judged by such criteria, most European states had quite simply failed. Nazi forces marching through Brussels, Copenhagen and Paris or ensuring the victory of an armed insurgency against the government in Madrid; mayhem, street violence and political assassination in Germany, Italy and much of Eastern Europe: all delivered an unequivocal message as to the inability of individual European states to fulfil the prime purpose of protecting their citizens.

The past failure and current weakness of nation states in 1945 is a prime well-spring of what was to become known as the 'European movement' dedicated to the broad notion of seeking to unite the states and people of Europe through some new entity. Such a new entity might have the size and strength to avoid the calamities which had befallen the post-1919 state system. It might also offer Europe a better basis for handling its changed relations with the rest of the world – both the super-powers and the former colonies. It would be fanciful to suggest that such ideas played a major role in the development of resistance movements during the later stages of the war, but they did feature in their political programmes. Certainly for many Europeans there was a sameness of historic experiences during those years, which also witnessed reconciliations between some historic ideological enemies. Prior to 1939 the divide between liberal, secular, republican forces and groups supportive of the church had been central to the basic political cleavages in many European countries. One of the key political forces in 1945 – Christian Democracy – was dedicated to bridging that divide. Extolling a broad Christian heritage Christian Democrat parties unequivocally accepted secular democratic states and recognised the need for central intervention to promote social and economic welfare. These parties rapidly reached positions of dominance in both Italy and West Germany. Their French equivalent, the MRP, played a key role in government in the early years after 1945. In Belgium, the Netherlands and Luxembourg (Benelux), Christian Democrat parties held similar positions. A shared Christian legacy gave these parties the rudiments of a trans-national ideology which almost by definition distanced them from the traditional, often nationalist right. Christian Democracy was to become closely identified with the 'European movement'.

An immediate political problem confronting Europe was the future of Germany. At one level German aggression seemed at the heart of a series of wars. Logically there was an incompatibility in seeking to heap all the blame on Germany if it were also held that Nazism was the key culprit. Harking back to the 1920s offered mixed messages. The then victorious allies had alternatively sought to crush and to conciliate Germany but had ended by doing neither. In terms of economic potential Germany remained the strongest European country and despite war losses was much more populous than Britain, France or Italy. The Iron Curtain which was to fall over Europe cut Germany in two, but even this did not resolve the 'German problem'. In the narrower context of Western Europe, Britain and France faced exactly the same policy dilemma as in 1919 – to crush or to conciliate. The German problem lay at the very heart of any discussion about European unification and both were significantly affected by the division of the continent.

From 1945 onwards there is a close umbilical link between the German problem and what we may term the 'European idea'. It rapidly became obvious that there was no possibility that the Soviet Union would allow the countries it controlled in Eastern and Central Europe to join in any free association with the West. However, if a united Europe comprised only the western part of the continent, it could hardly be a reality without Western Germany. On the other hand a united Europe also offered one possible route for containing German strength. These considerations were reinforced by a further factor. Whatever the historic basis for fears of Germany on the part of its immediate neighbours, in the context of 1945 the Soviet Union and Red Army constituted a potentially much more dangerous threat. The apparent immediacy of the new threat ultimately determined Western European response to the classic policy dilemma concerning Germany.

The weakness of Europe's nation states and their need to find a solution to the problem of Germany are key features in the development of European integration. Equally important was the state of international politics. The division of Europe, whether promoted, sanctioned or merely legitimated by Yalta, did not resolve the potential for conflict between the two new super-powers. Nor in the period 1945–50 did the alignment of the frontier between East and West seem to offer any guarantee of long-term stability. By 1948 the only continuing partnership between the allies was in Austria. Almost every other country was clearly in one or other sphere of interest/influence.[2] Germany had simply been split into two and the Soviet Union had attempted to squeeze the other occupier out of Berlin. The Communist take-over in Czechoslovakia – alone in Central and Eastern Europe it had operated a democratic party system throughout the period from 1919 to 1939 – and the crises over Communist participation in the French and Italian governments suggested to the West that the Soviet Union was still basically expansionist. The states of Western Europe were finding themselves increasingly dependent on the

USA for both economic aid and military protection. Unification offered Western Europe a means of strengthening itself against both super-powers. There was some suggestion of an alternative ideology. In post-war France the soubriquet 'third force' was attached to the potential alignment between the Socialists and the MRP. It was not difficult, although it was always a fantasy, to extend the idea to the point of envisaging Europe as some kind of 'third force' between the two super-powers.

The central argument of this chapter rests on the idea that unification was a specific response to a series of problems which confronted a group of countries in Western Europe in the immediate aftermath of 1945. Fifty years later it is easy enough to praise or condemn those who propagated the 'European idea' as idealists, but such an epithet is largely meaningless. The statesmen and leaders concerned were seeking new methods of handling practical problems. They were national politicians seeking what they considered the national interest. It is interesting to contrast the views of Harold Macmillan who was to be Prime Minister when Britain first applied to join the Community, with those of Edouard Daladier, who had been French Prime Minister at the time of Munich. According to Macmillan:

> The most important motive behind the movement for European integration is the need to attach Germany permanently to Western Europe, but in such a manner that she cannot dominate it. This is as much a British as a continental interest. After all, we have fought two wars about this in one generation.[3]

Daladier occupies a niche in history as a supporter of appeasement of Germany before 1939, but years later he proclaimed his unswerving opposition to the European idea: 'When they say Europe, they mean Germany, and when they say Germany, they mean greater Germany.'[4] Although Macmillan was only ten years younger, there is a generational clash inherent in these views, but both politicians have seemingly assessed lessons from history in formulating a response to the major issue of the post-1945 period. The controversy is about the practicalities of power politics rather than about political ideals. As national politicians, each was concerned with the national interest, and on this occasion the the Briton seems much more far-sighted and clear thinking.

Like every political movement, that espousing European unification needed a vibrant mythology to help persuasion and it was not above inventing a certain amount of pre-history. Of course, myths do not have to be true and can appear in strange places! Thus one major

French survey of European history – admittedly written from a highly critical standpoint – proclaimed that 'Europe began in unity: it is older than the nations of which it consists'.[5] This is nonsense. Most of Europe's history has revolved around conflict between different groups – tribal, religious, national. Past periods of unity have been transient and have resulted from conquest. Much has been made of cultural, religious and social linkages between national elites, but these do not amount to any kind of united Europe.

Efforts have been made to boost the significance of a variety of references to notions of European unity by writers as disparate as the Abbé de Saint-Pierre and Goethe and by political activists such as Mazzini and the Cobdenite free traders. Immediately after the First World War Luigi Einaudi, who was to become President of Italy after the Second, wrote a series of articles advocating federalism rather than the League of Nations as a solution for Europe's problems. In the 1920s Count Coudenhove Kalergi established Pan Europe as a campaigning organisation. He presumably won over French Prime Minister Aristide Briand, who produced a vague proposal for a European constitution. Prior to the 1939 war more organisations came into existence, all at the time quite uninfluential. The period of pre-history was, though, to end with a powerful gesture linking it to the central, practical politics of the post-war period. Confronted with the imminent collapse of France in 1940 the British government proposed 'a declaration of indissoluble union'. Instead of two nations there would be 'one Franco-British union'. Whether the gesture was idealistic or merely quixotic, it reflected Britain's desperation to keep France in the war against Germany. As a piece of *realpolitik* it provides a link to the future: the truth is that neither Churchill's 1940 offer nor the rest of this pre-history has any specific relevance to the post-1945 course of European integration.

The real history of the European movement begins with a plethora of now mostly forgotten organisations active in the immediate post-war period in promoting the concept of unification. The historian Alan Milward puts forward a powerful argument to deny any real link between all these movements and the actual process of European integration:

> these ill-matched movements were of little importance ... in the political life of their own countries .... The European Unity Movement which they eventually formed in 1947 appears to have had practically no influence on the negotiations for the Treaty of Paris three years later.[6]

The relationship between ideas and actions is always complex and frequently obscure. Milward is perhaps a good antidote to some who give exaggerated importance to the activities of these various European pressure groups. However, what is true is that once they came together in 1947 to form what was to become the European Movement they acquired sufficient mass to have an impact on the ebb and flow of contemporary ideas. Membership, although a loose concept, included a number of significant political figures in a variety of European countries.[7]

There is one final aspect of the motivations for seeking European integration which is worthy of some analysis and that is the argument of scale, or, put more bluntly, the attractions of sizeism. It was easy in 1945 to equate success with size. Europe's political failures could be attributed to smallness; the military victory over Germany could be accredited to the sheer size of the new super-powers. The USA and the USSR seemed to be the future. It was equally assumed that in the Far East the advantage was now with China rather than Japan. The early literature of European integration is full of references to size as a key determinant for economic success. In most cases they were simple assertions. There were some major economic studies of the advantages of scale, but there was a tendency simply to take the case as proven. It was assumed that there was a direct relationship between size and economic potential/success. It was equally taken for granted in the immediate aftermath of 1945 that the new economics incorporating Keynesianism could predict and plan growth and prosperity. This was a key underpin for policy prescriptions in all Western countries. Arguments for a united Europe could fit readily into that context. Finally it is worth making the point that Britain in no way repudiated the size argument. Britain hoped to take advantage of large markets and consequent large-scale production through preservation of the Empire/Commonwealth and links with the USA. For nearly two centuries this had been the basis for Britain's economic prosperity, whilst its involvement with Europe had been dominated by war. Such considerations were the initial basis for British opposition to European integration. Policy makers saw Britain as the intersecting point of three circles – Empire, North Atlantic and Europe. Integration with the latter would undermine this unique position. There was an automatic and implicit assumption that Britain's choice would determine the outcome of any move towards European integration. Little consideration seems to have been given to the prospects and implications of an integration process which excluded Britain.

2 The context for integration

The previous chapter examined the state of Europe in the immediate aftermath of the Second World War and sought to evaluate early motivations for unification. The chronology of events will be resumed in Chapter 3. The scope and purpose of the current chapter is to place the movement towards European integration within a wider, more theoretical, context. The first two chapters are thus both concerned with setting the scene but from different angles.

From a political science perspective one problem of writing about European integration is that it represents a single phenomenon. Some of the earliest writers in the 1950s sought to construct a new political theory which would explain the process of integration beteen states and which would have a wide applicability. The problem was that they sought to do this on the basis of a single process involving the inter-relationships of just six countries over a very short time span and conditioned by a very specific context. The founder of this approach was Ernst Haas. He and his followers[1] offered some brilliant insights, but any general theory was ultimately of limited value. Within a few years, the context had changed. This inevitably affected the process: thereafter attempts to construct any kind of general over-arching integration theory were more or less abandoned.

As a process European integration is now nearly half a century old and it has generated a considerable amount of literature. Whilst some writers have occasionally used integration theory as a reference point, most have preferred to concentrate on empirical data. Remarkably little of the literature which examines the implementation of the treaties and the working of the European institutions has re-examined a context which has undergone a series of changes culminating in a revolutionary shift in the period since 1989.

Many writers adopt the approach of giving a blow-by-blow account of how integration reached its present state – from the Hague to Maastricht. They present the progress of integration as a sort of seamless web which has apparently transcended the difficulties of the 1960s and 1970s: for them, union in the nineties is a clear continuation of integration in the fifties! This approach has even on occasions given rise to what could be described as a 'Whig' interpretation of contemporary Europe replete with heroes and villains. Such an interpretation postulates the European Community[2] as the embodiment of progress and enlightenment: Monnet, Hallstein and Delors are 'heroic' figures fighting against such obscurantists or 'baddies' as de Gaulle and Thatcher. In complete contrast, there is perhaps inevitably a small body of revisionist literature which, in deploring the whole process, ignores the economic and technological context which has driven so much of it forward.

The present study re-examines the continuing process of European integration by placing it in a series of contexts – the historical legacy, world politics, economics and technology. They have throughout had a critical impact on European developments and the course of integration. Attention will also be paid, where relevant, to the ebb and flow of national politics. Parties, issues and personalities – particularly in the major Western European countries – have inevitably had a significant impact on the Community.

Although contemporary Europe is the prime focus, understanding the essentially European phenomenon of integration is impossible without consideration of the impact on the continent of world factors. Subsequent chapters of this book will consider in turn three periods of time but without placing any specific chronological dividing line between them. A conclusion will look at the future of European Union at the end of the century. In each period developments in European integration will be related to the changing external and internal contexts.

The initial, or first, period starts immediately post-war, runs through the 1950s and peters out in the 1960s. The outstanding features are the emergence of the world super-powers and the impact of the Cold War in its active phase; economic devastation wrought by the Second World War; and the political weakness of nation states – particularly those that had undergone military defeats, occupation and/or internal fascist governments. Above all, Europeans had to grapple with one major, specific problem, already discussed in the previous chapter – namely, Germany's future role in the continent. In a different era – half a century on – it is all too easy to understate the enormous impact of the 'German problem' on the preoccupations of European leaders in the 1940s and the decisive impact it had on the emergence of the Communities. The political imperative of a solution is crucial to an understanding of how the original six came together, why they agreed to the creation of the European Coal and Steel Community (ECSC) and even proposed a European Defence Community (EDC). It equally helps to explain the almost immediate relaunching of the Community concept after the EDC failure.

The path and purpose of European integration were defined from the outset by a number of clear and specific constraints – internal and external. During this phase the continent was divided and the geographic boundaries for future integration or co-operation determined by external factors beyond the control of European governments. The Soviet Union was in effective control of Eastern and Central Europe. Countries in that large part of the continent would not be permitted to work with the democracies of Western Europe save on terms which would be quite unacceptable to the latter. The European Community was thus created as a child of its time against a background of political and economic imperatives conditioning the behaviour of its leaders. In deciding whether or not to join the Community, the states of Western Europe had to balance the relative impact of these imperatives on their own interests. The structure which emerged was the result of those decisions and also of the inter-play of a number of different concepts and approaches.

At this stage it is worth digressing from the overall theme to introduce a number of those concepts which are so important in understanding the development of linkages between European countries. They became relevant to the politics of Europe during the first period and they will recur throughout this book. 'Unification' may at one level be defined simply as 'bringing together'. It is a vague, catch-all phrase underpinned by the notion of an evolving 'oneness'. 'Union' which results from this process of 'unification' will clearly have different gradations of closeness, perhaps conditioned by the means which are used. Thus 'inter-governmentalism' suggests co-operation between governments and states, bringing about a loose 'Union' based on aims and achievements rather than any merger. By way of contrast, 'supra-nationalism' suggests the emergence of a power or authority superior to that of national government or individual state. A 'Union' based on 'supra-nationalism' implies a gradual merger of governmental structures and processes as well as the adoption of a series of common goals. 'Integration' is the word used to describe the way in which this coming together takes place. It is a process rather than an end. To put it all another way, supra-nationalism and inter-governmentalism offer alternative structures for achieving unification and union. Whilst at various times different governments have supported one or the other as a preferred approach, they are by no means mutually exclusive. Indeed, as will be shown much later, what is now described as the 'European Union' is a judicious blend of the two,

A first critical or defining moment took place when six countries – Belgium, France, Germany, Italy, Luxembourg and the Netherlands – established the very first of the three European Communities – the European Coal and Steel Community. The Six opted for integration and supra-nationalism as the means of unification. However, there have throughout been two different approaches to 'integration' – the 'federalist' and the 'functional'. The 'federalist' approach looks to a new and complete constitution for Europe with a specific transfer of powers to the new 'supra-national' institutions. The basic characteristic of federalism lies in the existence of two tiers of government – one for the entire federation and one for its constituent parts (in this case the member countries). Powers are distributed between the two tiers by a written constitution or treaty. Each tier is fully autonomous and neither can remove, or interfere with, the powers of the other. Each will have an independent source of revenue with which to fulfil its role. There is, however, no prescribed blueprint for the exact distribution of those powers. It is sometimes suggested that where the preponderance of powers is with the constituent parts, the term 'confederalism' should be used.

The 'functional approach' is much less ambitious. Indeed, whereas federalism denotes a specific structure, functionalism is really little more than a concept or approach. It implies integrated decision-making structures operating within defined sectors, such as coal or agriculture. Within those sectors there will be 'supra-national' institutions but elsewhere governments and states retain their traditional authority. There is no new, over-arching constitutional settlement.

Throughout the history of the European Community there has been a lively controversy between the advocates of federalism and functionalism.[3] However, in the early 1950s the six countries which determined to pursue integration opted decisively for the functional route. This 'victory' of functionalism as the preferred means of further integration is crucial to understanding the context of the second period. Functionalism is not simply a variant of federalism. Federalism, if not directly aimed at the subordination of the nation state, does firmly place it in a reduced and less influential position.

Functionalism is, rather, the handmaiden to the nation state: it facilitates its strengthening,[4] and therein lies a fundamental paradox.
Unlike federalism, functionalism leaves formally intact the notion of national sovereignty. The nation states are still the major international players. The functionalist strategy was based on an assumption that interest groups would become locked into integration and that there would be a gradual shift of loyalties and expectations to the European entity.[5] This in turn would generate demand for further functional measures of integration. In this way the functional approach might ultimately arrive at the destination espoused by the federalists. The paradox is that, in so far as functionalism would help economic recovery, it would also strengthen the standing of nation states and possibly inhibit the shift in loyalties and expectations.

Perhaps this is the major characteristic of the second period. During the 1960s there was a revival of self-confidence on the part of nation states for whom economic recovery had helped promote political strengthening and stability. Doubts and questions about the shape and structure of Europe persisted side by side with claims about irreversibility in the process of integration. President de Gaulle was the first national leader in one of the Six to articulate these doubts and thus to draw attention to the fundamental dichotomy inherent in the functional approach.

Doubts about the future of European integration were reinforced during the second phase by a gradual but fundamental change in the nature of the Cold War: seemingly permanent – yet institutionalised, bureaucratised and ossified. Through the 1950s and into the early 1960s the Cold War had remained active, and it is possible to discern the ebb and flow of conflict as the two sides pursued the possibility of changing the front line. The Austrian state treaty and the construction of the Berlin Wall were differing manifestations of the conflict between the Eastern and Western blocs. By way of contrast, Soviet crushing of the Hungarian uprising and the Prague spring were internal events of the Eastern bloc. The Western bloc neither precipitated the events nor took action to prevent the denouement. East and West alike accepted the Iron Curtain as a frontier which neither any longer sought to cross. By the mid 1960s the Cold War in Europe was thus largely quiescent. It remained an external agent of integration – but a passive rather than an active one.

The changing face of the Cold War led to a different kind of ossification of the German problem, with a subtle change in its contours. In the first period Adenauer made a clear choice for integration with Western Europe rather than seeking reunification based on a deal with the Soviet Union. The relatively 'hot' Cold War placed the two Germanies in formally hostile camps. Ossification of the Cold War as a stable part of the international environment made it possible for Brandt to pursue a new Ostpolitik based on formal acceptance of two Germanies, with an attempt to improve relations between them. The importance of the Federal Republic as a key player in the process of Western European integration was unchanged, but in the 1970s and early 1980s it was beginning to seem more pre-determined than a matter of choice.

During the second phase or context the Community deepened and broadened in scope and membership. None the less, there is a sense in which European integration was on 'automatic pilot'. The Community had now become an accepted and seemingly permanent feature of the political structure of Western Europe. It is possible to argue that in the 1950s the very idea of a Community was revolutionary, offering as it did a new way of tackling issues of inter-state relations. But by the 1970s this revolutionary aspect or newness was tarnishing. The point is under-scored by the fact that some new member states – Britain and Denmark – still did not accept the supra-national route to unification. Officially – from a Community perspective – they had changed their view to gain admittance. The reality was slightly different: the Community they were joining represented continuity rather than ongoing change. The ossification in East–West relations and the Cold War thus spread to the Community and became an important charac-teristic of the time. In consequence, few fundamental questions were raised about the nature of Western institutions. Whereas during the first phase the very notion of the European Community might have been revolutionary, during the second it was part of the accepted and recognised order.

This ossified external context has now been swept away by a series of events which started almost imperceptibly during the latter part of the 1980s and have effectively ushered in a third period. The disinte-gration of the Soviet Empire, the re-emergence, creation or re-creation of a string of separate nation states in Central and Eastern Europe and the reunification of Germany have beached the Cold War as a factor in European integration. The active external threat from the Soviets was a key ingredient in commencement of the integration process. Some of the theoretical writings refer to the idea of 'external federators'. For post-war Europe the Soviet Union fulfilled this role. Ironically, its removal can only raise uncertainties. There is a sense in which the collapse of the Soviet Empire has re-created the Europe of 1914, prior to the First World War: Russia has 'rejoined' the

European continent, within which Germany is potentially dominant. However, nation states were by no means the norm for Europe in 1914: Eastern and Central Europe was largely under the sway of three multi-national Empires. In that sense the emerging pattern of boundaries post-1989 has much more in common with 1919 and the Versailles settlement which ended the First World War. That settlement brought about the creation of a number of new states, frequently with artificial boundaries, but based – at least theoretically – on national identity. The instability of these states was one factor in the disasters which followed. Three-quarters of a century on, Europe has more putative nation states than ever: an odd juxtaposition with attempts at unification.

It is tempting to hail the re-appearance of 'Europe from the Atlantic to the Urals'.[6] However, any suggestion that there is now a single Europe adopting common principles as a basis for government is misleading in a number of respects. First of all, a half century of history cannot simply be swept aside. For some of the states and peoples of Eastern and Central Europe, domination by, or submergence within, the Soviet Union is their longest single experience in modern times as well as being the most recent. Second, there is a clear incompatibility between the development of a Community/Union in Western Europe and the wave of nationalism which is now the dominant ideology in the former Soviet sphere. Third, suggestions that changes in the East are simply restoring democracy and legitimate government are clearly facile given that for many new countries it is their first experience in modern times of independent statehood. In most cases there is simply no past history of democratic government. Fourth, there are few signs as yet of the emergence of permanent party systems in Central and Eastern Europe. The key political forces – civil rights groups which led the revolutions, mutating ex-Communists, nationalists – bear no resemblance to the established parties of Western Europe.

The re-appearance of the German problem in a more traditional context has significant implications for the rest of Europe. Until the end of the 1980s the external policy of the Federal Republic of Germany was conditioned by its exposed geographic position, its consequent reliance on the West and the continuing need to 'atone for the past'. A variety of constitutional and treaty arrangements limited sovereignty in defence issues, with consequent implications for foreign policy. As a result, West Germany was never able to match political influence to economic strength. Indeed, in this sense Germany in Europe was a paradigm for Europe in the world. A united Germany is potentially in a quite different position in the 'new' Europe. In terms of flows of people, goods and money Germany is again at the hub of the continent. To some extent fears of German domination may actually reinforce pressures for integration on its neighbours. However, there are also implications for the power balance inside the European Community.

The key event in the European Community in the 1980s was the signature of the Single European Act, discussed in Chapter 8. This seemed at the time a decisive break with the ossification and inertia which had characterised this second period. It was signed at a time when the old certainties still persisted: the ease of ratification demonstrates this. Within a few years those certainties were to vanish with the collapse of Communism and the Soviet Empire and the (re)emergence of Europe's new/old contours. The impact of the changing context can be readily illustrated by examining responses to the Maastricht Treaty on European Union, which was intended to consolidate the achievements of the Single European Act. Whilst the later agreement contains little which goes conceptually beyond the earlier one, its ratification was a long-drawn-out process with the final result in considerable doubt. Initial rejection of the entire treaty in the first Danish referendum could be likened in some respects to France's repudiation of the proposed European Defence Community near the beginning of the whole integration process. Both events will be discussed in detail later in the book. However, a general principle can be asserted that national repudiation of treaties and obligations entered into by governments is almost invariably a symptom of national uncertainty and government weakness. Thus France in the mid 1950s and Denmark at the time of Maastricht found it difficult to reconcile national identity with integration. Both had complex coalition governments, contending with traditions of parliamentary dominance over the executive.

The current, third phase is much hazier – its edges much fuzzier – than its predecessors. Old certainties seem part of a forgotten world. With no great ideological divides in Europe, pragmatic approaches to problem solving are in vogue. Integration continues to both deepen and widen. It has come to embrace ever more of the activities of the member states of what is now renamed the European Union, whilst more and more countries are seeking to join. This is partly a reflex from the previous contexts, but it is also important to recognise that in a shrinking world, social, economic and technological factors are faced with fewer restraints in the ways in which they influence political behaviour.

Time lags can be important in international politics. The previous paragraphs were devoted to the ways in which Europe and the world were changing whilst the Maastricht Treaty was being negotiated. Throughout this latter process the major concerns of Community leaders were focused on internal agendas. There is a sense in which the Maastricht Treaty embodies the sum of all past Community activity and all the thoughts and plans for future progress. 'European Union' – phrase or concept – had been an agenda item for nearly twenty years: the suddenness of its construction may in part have been a reflex action generated by the new uncertainties. Maastricht completed a process. The spirit of optimism characterising the signing of the Treaty also posited it as a basis for a series of new developments. However, the difficulties of the ratification process illustrate the new context and associated uncertainties as they impact on integration.

Ironically, whereas Western European responses to the ending of the Cold War have opened up doubts and questions, there has been no such reticence further East. There the question marks are basically internal – over the future shape and structure of regimes and political systems. In contrast, the Community/Union attracts, both because it radiates an apparent stability and as a contrast with past experiences. This is the major explanation for the plethora of new applications for membership, led admittedly by a group of predominantly West European countries – Austria, Finland and Sweden – political neutrals whose past exclusion had equally been a product of the Cold War.[7]

The last part of this book looks at future challenges facing the European Union in the light of both its historic development and the new external context. Although the external context which shaped the process of integration has changed irrevocably, the broad structure of the Union is little different from that of the Community which emerged under totally different circumstances. The additional super-structure which turned Community into Union reflects the logic of the established process and not the new context. There are fundamental issues about the appropriateness of the Community method and institutions designed for six contiguous countries at the height of the Cold War for potentially handling the problems of the vast plethora of states which now stretch from the Atlantic all the way to Russia, Ukraine, Byelorussia and Turkey. Simple insistence that the sole condition for membership is acceptance of the whole of what is known as the 'acquis communautaire'[8] is hardly an adequate response.

At the end of this second 'setting the scene' chapter it may be worth drawing attention yet again to the various purposes of this book – to give both a history of European integration, placed within a wider political and economic context, and an account of the structure and functions of the different European institutions. The linking of process and context is the key to explaining the evolution of the Community, its metamorphosis into the Union and possibly ultimately into a Federal Europe. This linkage will be the major preoccupation of Chapters 3, 5, 6 and 7. Chapters 4 and 8 will offer 'stand-alone' analyses respectively of the function and structure of the European Community and of the post-Maastricht European Union. Chapter 9 will take a forward look at Europe's future and will specifically seek to assess the prospects for a European federation.

3   The emergence of the Six

Reference was made in the first chapter to the plethora of pro-European campaigning groups active in the years immediately after 1945. These were paralleled by a series of actual and proposed organisations of different combinations of European states. They were all established in the context of promoting the vague concept of 'greater unity', but many were stillborn and others did not last. According to one slightly cynical commentator:

> Europe henceforward followed many paths but she got bogged down in them all. The Foreign Ministers of western Europe, like actors on a revolving stage which had got out of control, kept reappearing every few days, always playing a never-completed first act.[1]

Perhaps this is too bleak an assessment. In retrospect the period from 1945 to 1950 was critical in determining the course of subsequent developments. An over-view would divide the new organisations into three categories – economic, military/security and political. The major concern of this book is ultimately with those organisations which directly contributed to the drive for European unification. However, in those early formative years motivations for establishing organisations in all three categories were inter-twined. Even if the theme of unification was always to a degree present, the pragmatic needs of post-war construction were more significant.

The major new economic structure was the Organisation for European Economic Co-operation(OEEC), established in 1948 with an initial membership covering all Western Europe except Finland,[2] Germany and Spain. The Federal Republic of Germany participated from 1949. OEEC objectives were to organise the effective use of US economic aid, to ease trade restrictions and to operate as a clearing bank in processing payments between member states. The first major military/security structure was the Brussels Treaty Organisation, also established in 1948. It incorporated mutual defence arrangements between Britain, France, Italy and the three Benelux countries. In essence this meant acceptance by Britain of a commitment never formally given before the two great wars – namely, to defend other states in Western Europe against German aggression. The extent to which the thinking behind this treaty was dated is demonstrated by the fact that within twelve months it was largely superseded by NATO, which incorporated the historic and major commitment by the USA to defend Western Europe against the Soviet threat.

By way of contrast, the first major political organisation, the Council of Europe, with a wide Western European membership, came into being with the specific aim 'to achieve a greater unity between its members'. The difficulty confronting the Council lay in the means by which such an aim was to be achieved – 'by discussions of questions of common concern and by agreements and common action in economic, social, cultural, scientific, legal and administrative matters'. This was so vague as to be virtually meaningless: in practice there was nothing in the Council structure which facilitated action as distinct from talk. Formally inhibited from even considering defence issues, the Council equally lacked the effective power to determine economic questions.

Political organisations lacking competence to handle military and economic issues can be likened to 'Hamlet without the Prince of Denmark'. Creation of the Council could be hailed as a first step towards uniting Europe. However, its statute reflected diplomatic inter-play between proponents of integration (particularly France and Benelux) and opponents (particularly Britain and the Scandinavian countries). For the latter, the separate resolution of economic and military/security issues through the OEEC and the Brussels Treaty offered a means of avoiding the creation of strong political organisations with supra-national aspirations. It is a tangled web, and our same 'cynical commentator' was only being slightly unfair in his acid comment that the new 'organisations exchanged delegations ... with the others, and co-ordinating committees were set up, the number of which grew in geometrical progression with the foundation of each new organisa-tion'. It all led to 'a sham world of supra-national organisations tirelessly organising their own activity in the void'![3]

During the period 1945–50 Britain retained enormous potential influence in Europe, partly as a result of war-time memories and partly because it still seemed to be a great power. Despite the disparity in economic and military strength, Britain remained the chief overseas ally of the USA. A much more equal partner than was later the case, Britain in the immediate aftermath of the war still had some influence on the evolution of US global policy. The world view of British policy formers based on the three circles mentioned in the first chapter retained some relevance in the world of the late 1940s. Its weakness lay in a failure to realise the speed of change – the ever-growing disparity in power between Britain and the USA and the implications of the evolution of the British Empire into a Commonwealth of independent states free to pursue their own interests. The British government felt that all the real European issues could be dealt with through the OEEC and NATO, which were responsible respectively for economic and military/security questions. On this analysis the Council of Europe was no more than a sop to Euro-enthusiasts. With the advantage of hindsight we can see that the British government was to some extent misled by the sheer weight of propaganda activities undertaken by the pro-unification groups referred to in the first chapter. This resulted in a complete failure to understand the real motivations of other governments which espoused unification based not so much on ideological commitment but rather on hard-headed assessment of their own national interests. The Council of Europe had theoretically wide competencies but no power of action. An ultimately sterile debate on the need for the Council to be endowed with 'limited competence but real powers' was a key part of the background to the emergence of the Six – in effect a breakaway group – and the creation of their first structure, the European Coal and Steel Community.

On 9 May 1950 French Foreign Minister, Robert Schuman, issued a declaration which had in effect been drafted by Jean Monnet.[4] Relatively little space in this book will be given to individuals, but Jean Monnet has to be an exception. As an international civil servant he worked for the League of Nations after the First World War. His commitment to seeking new structures which could more effectively avoid international conflict was to underpin his work for European integration after the Second World War. In successive stages of his career he helped convert key French opinion formers within and outside the government to the notion of a united Europe, became the first President of the High Authority of the European Coal and Steel Community and finally founded and led the Action Committee for a United States of Europe designed to convert opinion formers throughout Western Europe. The ultimate goal may have been a federal Europe, but Monnet was a functionalist. He never showed much interest in parliamentary assemblies, referendums or elections, preferring to work on elites and opinion formers. To a large extent the construction of the European Community was along lines inspired by Monnet.

In so far as the Schuman declaration can reasonably be considered as marking the chronological beginning of the European Community, it is worth quoting complete:

> The contribution which an organised and active Europe can make to civilisation is indispensable for the maintenance of peaceful relations. France, by championing during more than twenty years the idea of a united Europe, has always regarded it as an essential objective to serve the cause of peace. Because Europe was not united we have had war.
>
> A united Europe will not be achieved all at once, nor in a single framework; it will be formed by concrete measures which first of all create a solidarity in fact. The uniting of the European nations requires that the age-old opposition between France and Germany be overcome: the action to be taken must, first of all, concern France and Germany.
>
> To that end, the French government proposes that immediate action be concentrated on one limited but decisive point. The French government proposes that the entire Franco-German production of coal and steel be placed under a joint High Authority, within an organisation open to the participation of other European nations.

Beyond the rhetoric, two aspects of the declaration are of particular importance. The Franco-German relationship was seen as the key to European unity. In the final paragraph Schuman implied that joint arrangements could even start with those two countries alone, although there is a clear implication that others would follow. In fact, the Schuman declaration marked the beginning of what was to become the Franco-German axis in European affairs. It is no exaggeration to claim that henceforth the course of European history, and with it the prospects of unification, revolved around the ebb and flow of that relationship. Second, Schuman implicitly repudiated any suggestion of an immediate 'constitution' for Europe. Rejection of a single framework and concentration on the 'limited but decisive point' was to become the hallmark of what became known as functionalism.

The French Foreign Minister invited other governments to join in constructing what was to become the European Coal and Steel Community (ECSC). Germany agreed on the same day as the declaration and it soon became clear that Italy and the three Benelux countries would also accept. Attempts were made by Monnet in particular to try to persuade Britain to participate, but by 31 May the Labour government was declining to enter 'into an advance commitment to pool coal and steel resources and to set up an authority, before there had been full opportunity of considering how these important and far reaching principles would work in practice'.

These words characterise contemporary British attitudes. In rejecting supra-nationalism, successive British governments[5] consistently objected to seeking to determine principles before considering details. This is much more than a matter of semantics. The dichotomy between 'British pragmatism' and the 'Community method' continues even now to be a source of division within the Community/Union. At about the same time as the 31 May statement, the Labour Party published a statement entitled 'European Unity'. Whilst reiterating the government's approach to Monnet's ideas, the statement also confirmed Britain's geo-political outlook: 'in every respect except distance we are closer to our kinsmen in Australia and New Zealand than we are to Europe'. Indeed, the statement could have added the USA to Australia and New Zealand. It is worth making the point that the USA, whilst broadly favourable to moves towards European unity, was not at this stage necessarily pressing for British participation.

The negotiations which were to produce the European Coal and Steel Community took place without Britain. There is plenty of evidence that the French government genuinely wanted British involvement. It is possible to argue that ever since 1918 France had shown some reluctance to take significant initiatives in Europe without British participation. Given the primacy for Britain of its world/transatlantic/Empire/Commonwealth links, this had not infrequently occasioned paralysis in French policy. By 1950 France was ready to contemplate grasping on its own the nettle of relations with Germany. None the less the conflicting pressures remained. Successive French governments accepted the need to reach a new accommodation with Germany, but were nervous of going too far without British involvement. It is often argued that Britain could have taken the lead in Europe had it only been willing to join the Coal and Steel Community. There is much evidence that France wanted Britain at the very least to 'hold the ring'. British reluctance meant that throughout the 1950s French policy would continue to be pulled in two opposing directions, although by the end of the decade the die would be cast. It was almost like severing an umbilical cord!

The ECSC Treaty was signed in April 1951 in Paris. Ratification took longer than negotiations, but this was completed by the end of July 1952. The aims and objectives of the treaty can be analysed at two distinct and contrasting levels. Formally the treaty is concerned with the establishment of a common market for coal and steel, managed by joint institutions on the basis of agreed policies. These would cover production, consumption, prices, trade, expansion and development and also social and economic conditions affecting those working in the industry. Whilst such commitments were of themselves a radical departure in inter-state relations in Europe, they applied in practice to only a limited sector of the economy. On the other hand, in contrast to the Council of Europe, the new Community, with its supra-national institutions, had a clear capacity to take and implement decisions. The integration process had begun.[6]

The specific commitments accepted by the Six are placed in a very much wider context by the preamble to the treaty and by article 2. The latter envisages the ECSC contributing to economic expansion, growth in employment and increases in the standard of living. The preamble goes far beyond even these general objectives. After references to the need for world peace and the contribution Europe can make comes a key sentence. The Six have

> resolved to substitute for age-old rivalries the merging of their essential interests; to create by establishing an economic community, the basis for a broader and deeper community among peoples long divided by bloody conflicts; and to lay the foundations for institutions which will give direction to a destiny henceforth shared.

It is powerful language and conveys an explicit commitment to ongoing integration. For the framers of the Treaty of Paris the management of coal and steel was visualised as simply the means to a wider and clearly more important end.

In the forty-plus years which have elapsed since the treaty came into force, progress has been highly uneven, and it has certainly been far from automatic. As it turned out, the period 1950–52 was an early high-water mark for European integration. It is a central thesis of this book that the integration process has throughout been conditioned by external forces, particularly a series of changing contexts. This was dramatically illustrated in the summer of 1950. Within a few weeks of the Schuman declaration, North Korea invaded South Korea. This was to be the only occasion during the Cold War when a Communist state launched a direct military attack on a non-Communist country. It was perhaps a defining moment in post-war history, for the USA inevitably assumed the role of leading world policeman in entering the war on the side of the South, although in the name of the United Nations. Already the USA had increasingly taken on previous British commitments in various parts of the globe. The US response to the Korean war was to seek help in carrying out these varied commitments. In Western Europe this necessitated a greater local defence contribution and this in turn had to imply German rearmament.

As has already been shown, the other nations of Western Europe were well aware of the need to normalise relations with Germany, but it did not follow that they were prepared to accept all the consequences. The reality is that in 1950 European public opinion was simply not ready for the re-creation of a German army along the lines suggested by the USA. This is the background to a proposal by French Defence Minister Pleven for a European Defence Community (EDC) incorporating a European army with Germany as a full participant. This linkage of the popular cause of integration with the unpopular notion of German rearmament seemed peculiarly suited to the times. The succession of events from the Hague Congress and the emergence of the European Movement through the founding of the Council of Europe, the launching of the Schuman plan and the signature of the Treaty of Paris establishing the ECSC down to the launching of the planned EDC seemed to justify what almost amounted to 'Europhoria'. Pro-European parties, particularly the Christian Democrats, were strongly entrenched in the governments of all six members of the nascent Community. Given the early welcome by Winston Churchill for the concept of a European army, some even hoped for British participation after the Conservatives won the 1951 election and he became Prime Minister.

The air of unreality persisted when late in 1952 the foreign ministers of the Six asked the parliamentary assembly of the Coal and Steel Community to draft a treaty for a European Political Community. This work was completed within six months and the resultant draft handed to ministers. Not surprisingly, major national differences were revealed in the twelve months of negotiations which followed, and this led to a significant watering down of the assembly's proposals.[7] All this was putting the cart before the horse with a vengeance! The EDC and a European army might have been a viable proposal if there had already been in existence a strongly articulated and coherent political structure. One year of joint management and policy making in the coal and steel sectors was hardly an adequate substitute.

Meanwhile, the political situation in France had in fact changed dramatically with the 1951 elections. General de Gaulle, France's wartime liberator, had formed a new right-wing nationalist party which would certainly not welcome the submergence of the French into a European army. At the 1951 elections Communists (who were totally opposed to German rearmament) and Gaullists between them won 47 per cent of the vote. It is doubtful whether pro-Europeans within and outside France fully grasped the significance of these events. Succeeding French governments based on broad coalitions of centre parties lacked all capacity for initiative of any kind, whilst the automatic majority for measures designed to promote European integration had disappeared. By the time the French assembly at last got round to considering and rejecting the EDC in August 1954, the outcome was inevitable. It is, however, worth adding one point, apart from the fact that the Korean war which had occasioned the controversy ended in 1953. Amongst those who voted against the EDC were some who clearly would have been more willing to go with the proposal had it included Britain. It follows that the historic pull of Britain on French policy towards Germany had still not wholly disappeared. Events of the next few years would complete that particular process.

Meanwhile, the issue of German rearmament still had to be resolved. During the period of French indecision, US Secretary of State John Foster Dulles had somewhat unsubtly, if inconsequentially, threatened an 'agonising reappraisal'. After the vote in the French Assembly, Britain successfully placed itself centre stage in Europe – possibly for the last time – by proposing a re-negotiation of the Brussels Treaty which now mutated into the Western European Union. Germany regained its sovereign status and with it the right to an independent army (the one thing the French had been so anxious to avoid), although it was formally inhibited from manufacturing or owning atomic, bacteriological or chemical weapons. Germany would be a full member of both the Western European Union (WEU) and NATO. To reassure France, Britain guaranteed to keep forces on the continent. Thus the USA's requirement for a German contribution to European defence against the Soviet Union led to a British army permanently based in Europe, which was in a psychological sense to protect France against Germany.

The collapse of the EDC project led inevitably to some deflation in what was referred to earlier as the 'Europhoria' of the early 1950s. The emergence of the WEU as a new vehicle for resolving Europe's political difficulties seemed momentarily to imply that the Six simply could not go it alone without Britain. A further implication was that cooperation and inter-governmentalism would now be the basis for unity rather than supra-nationalism and integration. Undoubtedly this was the assessment of the British government, but it was to turn out to be even more inaccurate than had been the case before the Schuman plan.

In June 1955, only ten months after the French Assembly had voted against the EDC, the foreign ministers of the Six were meeting at Messina in Italy to start the process which was to lead to the establishment of Euratom and the European Economic Community (EEC). They concluded that 'the work of establishing a United Europe must be accomplished by developing common institutions, by a gradual amalgamation of the various national economies, the creation of a common market and the progressive co-ordination of their social policies'. In the light of what was to happen the following year at the time of Suez, it is particularly significant that the foreign ministers also asserted their belief that unity was 'essential if Europe is to retain its present position in the world, if its influence and radiance are to be restored'. The words are ungainly, but the motivation is clear.

The Six established a committee under the chairmanship of the Belgian Foreign Minister, Paul-Henri Spaak[8] to prepare a report. Britain was again invited to participate and did so until the end of 1955. The myth is that the detailed negotiations which took place in Brussels from June 1956 ran smoothly on the basis of a shared political commitment, leading to the Treaties of Rome, which established Euratom and European Economic Community. The reality was rather more complex.[9] Most of the major problems were raised by France. They concerned issues such as the nature of the transitional period before the customs union took effect and the measures of economic policy which would offer reassurance against German industrial domination; arrangements for agriculture; and overseas links with existing and former colonies. At one stage the latter issue threatened to torpedo the negotiations. The final outcome in the French National Assembly was by no means pre-determined and some still felt that France should not go ahead without Britain. The underlying reality was that France still had not finally made up its mind about the course of future policy. Significantly, it was another quite extraneous event which was to be decisive.

In 1956 the Egyptian government nationalised the Suez Canal, which had been co-owned in effect by Britain and France. That autumn Britain and France took military action against Egypt, only to be forced into ignominious retreat faced with censure by the United Nations and a virtual collapse of the transatlantic alliance. The Suez adventure and its outcome marked the end of the myth that any European powers were still in the same league as the USA and the USSR. However, the two European partners clearly drew contrasting lessons from the disaster. Never again would Britain take 'independent' action in foreign policy without first clearing it with the USA.

France drew precisely the opposite conclusion that there could be no automatic reliance on the USA. The policy implication was exactly in line with the approach of the foreign ministers at Messina as quoted above.

The EEC and Euratom treaties were signed in Rome on 25 March 1957. Ratification took place exceedingly promptly on this occasion, and the two new communities came into operation at the beginning of 1958. Only in France was there any significant parliamentary opposition. Given the then chaotic state of French politics, the normal inability of government to carry anything and indeed the imminent demise of the Fourth Republic, the size of the majority could be considered as a tribute to the strength of pro-European sentiment![10]

The long-term goals of the EEC seem much less ambitious than those of the ECSC, or at any rate the language has less hyperbole. There are no references to 'merging interests' or 'sharing destiny'. The Six 'determined to lay the foundations of an ever closer union among the peoples of Europe', but that apart the aims are expressed in matter-of-fact, prosaic terms:

> The Community shall have as its task, by establishing a common market and progressively approximating the economic policies of Member States, to promote throughout the Community a harmonious development of economic activities, a continuous and balanced expansion, an increase in stability, an accelerated raising of the standard of living and closer relations between the states belonging to it.

Clearly, the scope of the new Community would very much wider, its potential impact on the lives of Europeans much greater, than that of the ECSC. The EEC Treaty offers a judicious blend of *'laissez-faire'* economics and interventionism to promote social goals. The centre-piece of the Community would be a common market or customs union. Tariffs and other trade restrictions within the Community would be abolished, whilst there would be a common level of tariffs for goods coming from non-member countries. All this would take place in accordance with an agreed timetable specified in the treaty. There would be common policies for agriculture and transport; action to ensure fair competition and the co-ordination of economic policies. The treaty contains relatively few specific details as to the precise implementation of these commitments. The member states in effect 'agreed to agree': this process which became known as the 'Community method' is discussed in more detail in the next chapter. There were also provisions for a joint investment bank to help with the goal of economic expansion, a social fund to improve employment and promote living standards and the association of former colonies as a means of promoting economic development. It may be worth recalling Britain's original participation in the Spaak committee. Apart from antipathy to supra-nationalism, Britain had been unwilling to accept either a common external tariff or the proposed common agricultural policy, fearing that both would damage economic links with the Commonwealth. Britain was always theoretically willing to participate in any arrangements for removing barriers to intra-European trade. However, all treaty arrangements had to be definite and specific: there was no acceptance of the notion of 'agreements to agree'.

By way of contrast with the EEC, the scope of Euratom was very much more limited. It focused on peaceful uses of nuclear energy, and its major concerns were research, health and safety, supplies, security and trade. Unlike the Treaty of Paris, the Euratom Treaty had few ambitions outside its own sector, although the preamble does contain one article of faith: 'nuclear energy represents an essential resource for the development and invigoration of industry and will permit the advancement of the cause of peace'. There is a similar reference to world peace in the preamble of the ECSC Treaty. The link with the EEC is underpinned by a statement that the task of Euratom is 'to contribute to the raising of the standard of living in the Member States'.

The subject matter of this chapter has concerned the emergence of European integration in the period up to 1958. It is a period rich in development, with many important events. Earlier it was suggested that the US response to the Korean war was a 'defining moment'. This rather elusive concept was introduced at the beginning of this book. 'Defining moments' encapsulate what has gone before and determine the future. Key actors have a choice: determination of that choice is crucial. The outbreak of the Korean war was the one occasion when the 'Cold War' became 'hot'; Communist and non-Communist state armies fought one another openly and officially. The final result – a return to the *status quo* pre-invasion – helped usher in the ossification of the second phase of the Cold War. The Korean war also marked the USA's formal assumption of the role as world policeman. It was indeed a defining moment, with a clear indication of the secondary nature of Europe's internal concerns. German rearmament in the 1930s led to a world war. German rearmament in the 1950s was imposed on Europe by world events.

It is tempting to see the Suez fiasco as another such defining moment, especially in view of the suggestion that it was the final determinant of French willingness to accept the EEC. In fact Suez may be little more than a footnote to history, a further illustration of European nation state weakness. It is, however, possible to argue that the establishment of the EEC in 1958 was, at least in European terms, a defining moment. Six countries confirmed their resolution to continue with integration through supra-national activity even if that meant a major rupture in Western Europe. The EEC was concerned with a much wider span of activity than the ECSC, and the process set in motion turned out in practice, as it was intended, to be both ongoing and irreversible. In European terms it removed Britain from centre stage and gave primacy to a new Franco-German axis. Ultimately this has re-orientated the entire direction of European history. Over the centuries, hostility and conflict between France and various Germanic powers had been a dominant theme. Each had sought the support of Britain, whose policy had been to maintain some rough equality in the power balance. In so far as the late nineteenth century had seen a decisive shift in power towards Germany, it was inevitable that Britain found itself henceforth more frequently aligned with France. Formally this period was ushered in by the Entente Cordiale of 1904 and lasted little more than half a century. Signature of the Treaties of Rome signalled that Franco-German agreement would henceforth be critical to developments in Europe. Historically, British policy in Europe had been based on an assumption of discord between France and Germany: an entire era had come to an end.

The next chapter will examine the institutions and processes of the three European communities in detail, whilst the more chronological approach to the development of integration in response to the changing context will be resumed in Chapter 5.

4   The European Community

The ethos and purpose of the European Community reflect the circumstances of its inception. Specifically, there are three communities – the European Coal and Steel Community, Euratom and the European Economic Community. The term 'European Community' first acquired general usage either as EEC writ large or as an assertion that somehow the three were as one. By the merger treaty of 1965 they came to share their institutions, but legally they remained separate, a point still emphasised in the Single European Act of 1986. Ironically, it is only with the Maastricht Treaty on European Union that the term 'European Community' is given legal force and then amidst a certain confusion.[1] The term 'European Community' will none the less be used extensively in this chapter as a collective for the three communities. 'Community' institutions are those responsible for the three communities.

Each of the three communities has its own specific functions, but all are geared to the broad aim of uniting Europe. The Treaty of Paris establishing the ECSC looks forward to a 'broader and deeper community among peoples long divided by bloody conflict', whilst specifying that 'Europe can be built only through practical achievements'. The two later treaties are less ambitious in comparison: the EEC seeks to 'strengthen the unity of their economies', whilst Euratom aims at 'joint effort ... to create the conditions for ... a powerful nuclear industry'.[2] The scope of the EEC is much wider than that of the two sectoral communities, although it is worth bearing in mind that the ECSC does have competences in the social sphere. Essentially, though, the two sectoral communities were concerned with joint control, planning and management of particular spheres of economic activity, whilst the EEC was concerned with general economic integration embracing a customs union, right of establishment, capital movements, transport, competition, energy, commercial policy and social policy.

The six original members settled on a framework for common action which seemed particularly appropriate to the needs of the moment. Underlying the treaties are two key principles. These two principles are sufficiently important as to justify some detailed analysis.

The first principle is that the detail of problem solving is subordinate to the attainment of a shared political will. Solving problems is a function of, and *not* the route to, that shared political will. This approach contrasts with the kind of pragmatism usually preferred by British governments. The latter prefer to see shared political will as the result of success in problem solving. This difference in approach is not just a matter of semantics. In the last analysis it reflects a fundamental difference both of philosophy and, therefore, in the methodology of action. Characteristic of the approach adopted by the Six is the extensive use in various treaty texts of the concept of agreeing to agree, with the details being worked out at a later stage. This is the Community method to which reference was made in the previous chapter. It is worth bearing in mind that the principle of subordinating problem solving to the attainment of a shared political will, of agreeing to agree and indeed the entire notion of a Community method, reflect a very Gallic approach. It is important not to forget the key roles played by the two Frenchmen, Jean Monnet and Pierre Uri, in the construction of the treaties.[3]

The Six came together as a result of sharing a political commitment to bring about the unification of Europe: this is explicit in the first Community text, that of the ECSC, and implicit in the later texts. In negotiating the three communities they were determined not to be bogged down in detail. Their scheme was to establish joint mechanisms which would deal with detailed problems. A shared political commitment would be surety that the mechanisms could always deliver solutions. The Six made the operational assumption that commitment to the major long-term goal of unification would always be a more important national interest than any differences over what would in context be essentially ephemeral problems. It is easy enough to gauge the extent to which this reflected the spirit of the times. Nation states were still relatively on the defensive. In a real sense they needed the functional communities. The shared goal was simply too vital to be risked for any short-term national considerations, and in the last analysis no member state would expect it to be.

The second principle flows naturally from this and it has come to epitomise the very essence of functionalism. In a nutshell, efficient technocracy becomes the key determinant of effective government. It is worth returning for a moment to the Council of Europe from which the Six were breaking away in their quest for unification. The Council, like the Hague Congress before it, epitomised a kind of Estates-General approach to Europe. The key ideas would come from an assembly of parliamentarians representing the peoples of Europe. The problem was that there was no motor to turn talk into action. Jean Monnet's major contribution was to focus on the 'smoke-filled room' as the location for the essential business of European construction.

There is a clear link between these two principles. To use the language of Rousseau, the creation of the Community was an act of the general will of the member states and their populations. They were willing action to solve problems and this requires effective and efficient mechanisms. The key institutional innovation was to be an appointed, but unelected, political executive which would possess those special skills to guide the polity. Perhaps then there is a touch of Plato as well as Rousseau in the philosophy which spawned the Community, in that the job and person specifications for commissioners seem similar to those of philosopher kings! The political executive – High Authority in the ECSC and the Commission in the EEC and Euratom – acts in a technocratic manner. The guiding principle is that if the political will for solution exists there must be a technical means of resolving any issue.

It would be absurd to argue that those who worked out the detail of the treaties – Jean Monnet in the case of the ECSC, Pierre Uri for the EEC – were anti-democratic. However, not being parliamentarians they seemed to posit democracy as responsiveness to freely expressed popular will rather than the institutionalisation of mechanisms of accountability through elected representatives. Thus in the ECSC the High Authority was intended to be paramount. The ministerial committee was only added as an afterthought and the Parliamentary Assembly was almost devoid of power. It seems bizarre that this same Assembly, which was not directly elected and had so little role in the ECSC, should almost immediately be charged with drafting a statute for a European Political Community.[4]

The two principles permeate Community institutions to this day, and their limitations in the changing contexts of integration have been potent sources of problems and discontents. The shared political will to make integration and unification the supreme goal barely survived the coming into force of the treaties. In the 1960s France was to demonstrate a different sense of national priorities. Later Community members had by definition no historic sense of the period of automatically shared common political will: by the 1980s the perspectives of Britain and Denmark, two who joined later, were in radical counterpose to those of the original Six.

The supremacy of technocracy in the decision-making apparatus created an immediate, if unintended, democratic deficit. This mattered little so long as the institutions were operating within pre-defined parameters, fulfilling the original treaty aims on the basis of a shared will amongst a cosy club of six. Over the course of nearly half a century the club has grown much larger and more disparate, whilst the context within which it was initially created has undergone significant changes. There has often been insufficient shared political will to ensure success when the Community has sought to develop new areas of joint activity. Under such circumstances it is perhaps not surprising that the lack of effective democratic control has raised questions about the legitimacy of the Community itself.

The basic institutional pattern of the Community, which is the subject matter of this chapter, has been broadly unchanged since the treaties were signed in the 1950s and their institutions brought together by the merger treaty. As new members joined – Britain, Denmark and Ireland in 1973; Greece in 1982; Portugal and Spain in 1985; Austria, Finland and Sweden in 1995 – the mechanisms have been adjusted. In addition, there have been a series of actual amendments to enlarge the powers of the European Parliament. Not until the Single European Act and the Treaty on European Union were there any general reforms of the structure and these, as will be shown, were hardly sweeping. The formulation of this chapter is rather complex and requires explanation. It examines the basic institutional structure as it emerged from the three foundation treaties, takes into account various reforms prior to the Single European Act (1986), *but it is based on an assumption of the current (1997) membership.* A number of issues relevant to the respective powers of different institutions are explored in the contextual chapters which follow. To gain a full picture of the current institutional pattern, the present chapter should be read in association with Chapter 8 which deals with the Maastricht Treaty on European Union.

The structure of the three original treaties is critically determined by application of the two key principles – political commitment and effective technocracy. Assuming a shared, all-pervasive political will, the original Six felt only a limited need to fix the precise details of their future collaboration. There is a sense in which the treaties can be seen as almost *tabula rasa*, an open book for future developments.

The scope of the precise commitments originally undertaken by the Six was quite limited, applying to little more than the timetable for customs union implementation and the actual level of the common external tariff. On the other hand, member states entered into numerous 'agreements to agree' at a later date over vast sectors of economic activity, including agriculture, competition policy, energy and transport. This approach has also characterised subsequent enlargement treaties where key issues have frequently been left to the 'agreement to agree' process. It is worth repeating the point that this is central to what is called the 'Community method', and it is often cited as evidence for the alleged uniqueness of the entire European structure.

It is commonplace for international institutions to be charged with responsibility for monitoring implementation. The scope and purpose of the European institutions established by the founding treaties necessarily go much further. It is part of the ethos that the institutional structure is at least semi-autonomous from the decision-making structures of the member states. Precisely because of their responsibility to facilitate the details of the agreements which it has been agreed to make, the progress of integration is heavily dependent on institutional performance.

The policy-making and decision-taking capacity of the Community is a function of the interplay of three specific institutions – Commission, Council and Parliament – with a fourth, the Court, as the arbiter and supreme interpreter of the rules. Ultimately the Court determines both the limits of European as against national competence and the respective roles of the three institutions involved in taking decisions and making policy. However, the Court is not itself part of those processes and stands aside from the detail of the running of the Community. The initial power relationship between the three institutions was defined by phraseology used extensively in the EEC and Euratom treaties – 'on a proposal of the Commission and after Parliament has been consulted, the Council will decide'. Clearly, implementation of decisions would involve further elaboration of the power relationship, but there is an immediate implication of Council superiority and Parliament marginality.

COMMISSION

Although the Commission is not the major focus of political power in the Community, it is an obvious starting point for this institutional analysis. The Commission is clearly the most revolutionary of the institutions and it is frequently described as unique. Members are appointed for a four-year term of office by the national governments. Each country has one commissioner, but there is a second from Britain, France, Germany, Italy and Spain. The Presidency is decided by joint agreement of member states. The essence of the Commission's role is to oversee European integration. Once appointed, commissioners accept a 'European' brief and are formally inhibited from receiving national instructions. The Commission is collectively responsible to the European Parliament, but in the event of dismissal through a vote of censure any new appointments would revert to member states.[5] Underneath the Commission are some 14,000 civil servants grouped into a variety of departments. By national standards this is a very small number. Sometimes the Commission is criticised for alleged bureacracy: any potential truth in the accusation would have to relate to working methods rather than size. Individual commissioners supervise the working of particular departments and handle appropriate policy briefs. However, responsibilities in a legal sense are entirely collective. There is no equivalent of individual ministerial responsibility. Commissioners make use of a private cabinet[6] system to help in handling their individual portfolios and also to ensure that they keep abreast of all important Community activity. These cabinets are small but are normally extremely high powered. They operate in effect as 'eyes' and 'ears' for their commissioner and their abilities are likely to determine his/her degree of success. The Heads of Cabinet (Chefs de Cabinet) are significant Community actors in their own right and frequently operate as if they were deputy commissioners.

The Commission has six major roles – proposer, mediator, administrator, guardian, representative and European conscience. The first aspect of the Commission's work as proposer lies in initiating the process of reaching the agreements it has been agreed to make. The perceived advantage to the original Six of establishing a Community first and handling the problems thereafter lay in the establishment of joint institutions which could tackle the issues from an independent position outside the inter-state arena. The Commission is responsible for problem solution, although it is clearly dependent for success on the political will of the member states. This is to reach to the very heart of the relationship between Commission and member states, which also embodies the core of the decision-making structure. Commission proposals for resolving problems and progressing integration go the Council of Ministers. This is the formal forum for decision taking but also the arena in which different national interests compete, and it is discussed in detail below. If member states share the will to reach a solution and accept its broad lines, then the Commission's role is largely technical and probably not very difficult. However, where those preconditions of broad agreement amongst members do not exist, the Commission's role is much more difficult. As well as demonstrating the facility to come up with a whole variety of technical solutions, the Commission also takes on the political role of trying to create a shared will for agreement amongst member countries.

This facet of Commission activity is particularly important in another aspect of its work as proposer. Here the Commission is not so much concerned with the detail of the agreements it has been agreed to make, but rather with extending the scope of integration – moving into completely new areas. In these cases the Commission is even more dependent on the corporate will of member states. Sometimes the process is inspired and initiated by the Commission. The most outstanding example was the European Monetary System, which clearly went beyond the then scope of the Community. The Commission's work as proposer gave a kick start to this major extension of Community activity. It should be added that this was a relatively unusual case. The Commission usually needs a clear prior indication of commitment from the member states and their leaders, who tend to be the major actors in this process. This then creates a context for the Commission as proposer.

Once proposals reach the Council of Ministers, the Commission finds itself acting as mediator rather than proposer. The initial expectation was that given the over-riding commitment to integration, the Commission would be able to raise competing national perspectives to a higher level. In practice the Commission is frequently concerned with the lowest common denominator for agreement. This may mean that the Commission has to give priority to mediating some kind of agreement rather than trying to steer through its own original proposals. The task of mediation has grown ever more complex. In the early years the Commission was dealing almost exclusively with areas covered by 'agreements to agree', and sometimes the basic treaties offered useful outlines. Decision making is now increasingly focused on areas which had little or no coverage in the treaties. Where extensions to the scope of the Community are concerned, the Commission often lacks the weight to ensure success in its mediation efforts. In this respect the role of President of the Council (see below) has been enhanced.

The Commission's role as administrator is not straightforward. Once decisions are taken the Commission has an overall responsibility for implementation, but day-to-day administrative responsibility is usually in the hands of national authorities. This of course also explains why the Commission can fulfil its various roles with such a small staff. In effect the Commission is really concerned with ensuring and supervising implementation of decisions and legislation. This flows almost imperceptibly into the fourth role as guardian of the treaties and of the almost mystical 'acquis communautaire'.[7] The Commission has a clear and specific responsibility (under article 8 of the ECSC Treaty; article 155 of the EEC Treaty and article 124 of Euratom) to ensure that member states fulfil their duties under both the original treaties and subsequent legislation. The Commission may persuade, cajole, negotiate, but ultimately it has to take action in the event of non-compliance. It will be for the Court of Justice to give a ruling, and sometimes this may involve the Commission in further action.

The Commission as representative is a function of the Community as a world economic actor. As such the Community participates in international economic organisations and it has developed an extensive network of bilateral links with third countries including the ACP (Atlantic, Caribbean and Pacific) associates. The scope of external relations has been extended by the gradual development of political co-operation,[8] leading to an increasing representative role also for the President of the Council. However, for matters within the competence of the Community, the Commission is the normal external spokesman. It also sends and receives diplomatic legations.

The final role of European conscience is self-assumed rather than treaty-based. The Commission perceives itself as embodying both the Community and the European idea itself. There is a real sense in which the Commission is present at the Council as a kind of extra member save that it does not represent a specific state. When the members are considering deepening and widening the scope of integration it is invariably the Commission which presents the 'European' view. At one level the Commission has been remarkably successful in presenting itself to public opinion as the embodiment of the Community and the European idea. The drawback is that the Commission is then held responsible by national politicians and by the media for policy failures even when it is not really to blame.

The legal power of the Commission is not constant across all aspects of Community activity. There are differences enshrined in the original treaties. Whenever integration is extended to a fresh sphere of government activity, the exact future roles of the institutions have to be determined. The greatest variations affect the Commission as administrator. However, its overall place in the power nexus is clear. It is the archetype supra-national institution and in many ways it drives the integration process. Its performance is critical to the operation of the Community, but the Commission does not control the major levers of political power. Its support is a necessary, but never a sufficient, condition for progress.

COUNCIL OF MINISTERS

In contrast, analysts have found it much more difficult to come to grips with the Council of Ministers. It consists of ministerial representatives from member states and now meets for several days each week. Different ministers attend, depending on the business to be transacted. The Council is thus a collective term for various series of meetings but in effect there is a hierarchy with the foreign ministers at the apex. The work of the Council is prepared by the Committee of Permanent Representatives (COREPER), whose members are civil servants or diplomats. Each member state has an accredited ambassador or permanent representative to the Community. These permanent representatives are normally high-ranking, and high-flying, civil servants or diplomats based in Brussels. COREPER meets twice weekly, although one meeting is handled by the deputies to the permanent representatives. These meetings are a key part of the decision-making process since they effectively co-ordinate the entire process of national negotiation leading up to the Council taking its decisions. Initially this substructure of the Council developed outside the formal treaties. However, it was given a legal basis by the 1965 merger treaty.

The ministerial organ in the ECSC was very much an afterthought intended as a check on the dominant High Authority. In the two later communities it is given far more scope. Essentially, the Council takes decisions and it is the institution most subjected to national influences. It has been described as an inter-governmental organ and certainly it is a forum in which member states' interests are reconciled through the negotiating process in which the Commission participates. However, in a formal sense the Council is responsible for making laws: it has even been described as a legislature. On this analysis, the Community simply cannot work effectively unless the Council operates as a European institution. Indeed, the extent to which the Council acts as an integrated institution is one key performance indicator.

Member states assume the Presidency of the Council on a six-monthly rotation. The President is responsible for steering the business of the Council and to some extent of the Community as a whole. The Council has a considerable Secretariat, which includes many linguists and lawyers and is responsible to the President. However, the country holding that position is also required to commit a considerable invest-ment of national resources. As the years have gone by and the work of the Community has extended, the role of President has increased in significance and visibility. The President often plays a more important role than the Commission in harmonising national interests and also enjoys an increasing prominence as an alternative representative of the Community, internally as well as externally. Thus a member country charged with the Presidency is quite likely to set targets for the six months of office. The President, in the person of either the Head of Government or a Foreign Minister, will also appear before Parliament at the beginning of the term of office.

The treaties provide two principal methods by which the Council takes decisions – unanimity and a form of weighted majority voting. After four waves of enlargement,[9] votes are distributed as follows: France, Germany, Italy and the UK each have 10 votes; Spain 8; Belgium, Greece, the Netherlands and Portugal 5; Austria and Sweden 4; Denmark, Finland and Ireland 3; and Luxembourg 2. A majority requires 62 of the 87 votes. If the big five voted *en bloc* they would require the support of at least three more countries, whilst the minimum blocking minority has to consist of at least three countries. At the outset it was assumed that majority voting would gradually become the norm with only a few matters subject in a formal sense to individual veto. As will be shown in the next chapter, this assumption was an early casualty of the loss of automatically shared political will. Although the voting rules were never formally changed, the constitu-tion in practice seemed to evolve in the opposite direction to that anticipated until the balance was redressed by a general (unwritten) agreement at the time of the Single European Act. However, the anal-ysis is far from being straightforward. Voting rules are important in a legislature. Diplomatic skill and power politics are much more signifi-cant in understanding the process and outcome in a negotiating forum. The Council is a little of both.

Foreign Ministers are at the apex of the Council and their series of meetings was intended to provide overall policy co-ordination. However, the political will needed to resolve major controversies and to extend the scope of integration has to come from an even higher level, and this requires an input by Heads of Government. In time this necessitated the emergence of a new tier of authority – the so-called European Council – which for more than a decade operated outside the formal context of the treaties. The European Council, meeting three times a year, gave overall political direction to the Community and was crucial to all new initiatives. It was not incorporated into the formal mechanisms until the Single European Act in 1986. Well before that it had become a kind of superstructure for the Council just as COREPER was the substructure.

THE EUROPEAN PARLIAMENT

The third institution directly involved in the governance of the Community is the European Parliament. Since 1979 this has been directly elected, but according to different national systems. There are 624 MEPs – Germany has 99; France, Italy and the UK each have 87; Spain 64; the Netherlands 31; Belgium, Greece and Portugal each 25; Sweden 21; Austria 20; Denmark and Finland each 16; Ireland 15; and Luxembourg 6. However, from its inception Parliament has operated through party rather than national groups. The European Parliament, unlike most national equivalents, is not the political base for govern- ment. In practice, the gradual erosion of traditional party systems and cleavages together with increased membership have been factors helping to increase the number of recognised groups. On the other hand, two of the groups – the Socialists and the European People's Party (incorporating Christian Democrats and Conservatives) – are much larger than any of their rivals and can together dominate Parliament. With fifteen member states and a multiplicity of party groups, decisions require a considerable degree of consensus formation and coalition building. In this process the relationship between the two major groups is critical. It is no exaggeration to suggest that the smooth running of Parliament is a function of co-operation/conflict between the Socialists and the People's Party.

In the decision-making nexus Parliament's original, formal role was purely consultative. However, in 1970, after member states agreed that the Community should acquire its 'own' budget, it was generally accepted that there would have to be an increase in parliamentary power. This was brought about by a series of treaty amendments in 1975. Henceforth, Parliament would have the final word on certain categories of expenditure,[10] and it would have to give approval to the entire budget (in the absence of which that of the previous year would continue in force). These budgetary arrangements introduced the concepts of co-operation and co-decision: Parliament became a formal partner in decision taking in this one area. In due course the Single European Act and the Treaty of European Union began extending these new concepts into the legislative realm.

The other aspect of Parliament's work arises from its formal legal control over the Commission. The basis is a treaty article requiring the Commission to resign if a motion of censure is carried by a two-thirds majority. This establishes lines of responsibility and accountability from Commission to Parliament. The former attend meetings, answer questions and respond to debates. However, Parliament can only determine its own position on an issue: it does not have the power to enforce a position on the Commission. The motion of censure as originally conceived was somewhat of a blunderbuss, with limited practical use given that the member states alone appointed the Commission. In practice, it is highly unlikely that any Commission will represent the exact constellation and balance of political forces in Parliament. However, as will be shown in Chapter 8, the Treaty of European Union has now given Parliament a role in the appointment of the Commission.

EUROPEAN DECISION MAKING

Before looking at the last of the major institutions – the Court of Justice – it may be useful to set in context how the Commission, Council and Parliament interlock for decision-making purposes. The basic procedure was determined by the foundation treaties: it does not apply to the budget, which is discussed in Chapter 6, nor to legislation now covered by rules for co-operation and co-decision as determined by the Single European Act and the Maastricht Treaty. Outside these areas the major nexus for decision making lies in the relationship between Commission and Council. Formally, the process starts with the Commission's right to initiate a proposal. In fact, the origin of the proposal may lie elsewhere in the system – for example, with member states. The Commission makes a proposal, which is passed on to the Council together with an opinion of the Parliament. The Council invariably asks COREPER (the Permanent Representatives) to study the proposal, which they do in the presence of Commission representatives. COREPER straddles the Council work of decision taking. A dossier can be referred downwards to committees of national experts for detailed technical discussion, or upwards back to the Council itself for decision on issues deemed to be political. The nature of the Community is such that almost any issue can become politicised through pressures in national parliaments, media coverage and ultimately differences between member states. The system is geared to an assumption that there is always a potential technical solution to a political problem, although the whole process can be extremely time consuming. The actual agenda for Council meetings consists of 'A'

points and 'B' points. The 'A' category is where COREPER have
reached agreement or at least consensus and the Council is simply
formally nodding the items through. 'B' is for decision, and it is here
that the voting rules can at least hypothetically be significant. At all
stages in the process the Commission is involved: its relations with the
Permanent Representatives are, therefore, critical.

THE COURT OF JUSTICE

The last of the major institutions, the Court of Justice, stands somewhat aside from the routine context of decision making. The role of
the Court is to act as arbiter and referee, and it is not really part of the
governance of the Community. It is made up of one judge from each
of the fifteen member countries plus nine advocates-general (one from
each of the five larger countries with the others in rotation). The role
of the advocate is to prepare an independent opinion on the case for
submission to the panel of judges. The Court's functions flow logically
from the nature of the Community as quasi-federal and operating to a
treaty-based written constitution.

It is a critical requirement for any state or organisation based on
written texts that there be an ultimate authority to interpret the
'constitution'. This task falls to the Court, which is in this sense
guardian of the treaties. The federal nature of the Community is
expressed in a codified division of powers between the European institutions and member states. To ensure uniformity, any issues over
jurisdiction must be resolved at the higher or quasi-federal level. The
Court is concerned with both national and European law. The latter is
binding on member states and their citizens: it co-exists with national
law. Harmonisation is needed to insure against any incompatibility
between national and European laws. This can only be brought about
by action at Community level. In effect, the Court has the legal power
to rule on the 'legality' of national laws where they impact on areas
covered by the treaties or subsequent Community legislation. As
supreme constitutional authority, it falls to the Court to determine
who has the right to legislate in any particular sphere. As harmoniser,
it can in effect declare invalid any national laws which in European
terms are deemed 'unconstitutional'. Equally, though, it can rule out
European laws where it deems that legislative powers still belong to the
member states.

It hardly needs stating that the Court's ability to fulfil its functions
depends totally on willingness by the member states to accept its jurisdiction. The Community is founded on law in the shape of a series of

inter-state treaties and a great deal of subsequent legislation. The central authorities lack any ultimate power of sanction and are in a real sense dependent on the member states. They are required to uphold and enforce European law in a national context and to accept in their own actions and behaviour the decisions of the Court. The hypothetical question may arise as to what can be done if a member state refuses to accept this jurisdiction. The first answer must be that this would undermine the entire basis on which the Community has been constructed. It is an article of faith that there will always be sufficient shared political will to ensure that this does not happen. Presumably an offending member state could in the event of refusal to accept the law be subjected to sanctions by other members, or even expelled. Resort to such procedures would, though, imply the breakdown of the Community system and the breakup of the Community itself. One possible conclusion is that Europe is establishing a legal system which is genuinely founded on consent.

The notion of national political institutions accepting the ultimate political authority of what becomes in effect a constitutional court raises no new principles for the governments of a large majority of member states. In most democratic systems there is nothing inherently unusual about the notion of a supreme legal authority declaring invalid executive acts of government or parliamentary legislation. Sometimes this is based on a constitutional approach which vests sovereignty in the people. Various powers are granted by or on behalf of the people to a variety of executive, legislative and judicial organs which co-exist in accordance with a written constitution. Britain's legal and constitutional approach is very different. In Britain, sovereignty is formally vested in Parliament – in effect, in the House of Commons, which is normally controlled by a government with a majority of seats. Parliament can legislate on any matter it chooses, but it cannot bind any successor parliament. Each parliament is free to enact its own legislation. Governments must act within that legislation, but can usually use a parliamentary majority to pass new laws if there are problems with the courts. The Community has thus changed the British constitution in a very fundamental way. Indeed, for Britain, this is one of the most revolutionary features of membership.

There is another major innovation, although this affects all member states equally, and this arises from the direct applicability of the Community law. The key determinant is in article 189 of the EEC treaty: 'A regulation shall have general application. It shall be binding in its entirety and directly applicable in all Member States.' This was reinforced at an early date by the Court of Justice determining that direct applicability would also apply to certain treaty articles themselves.[11]

On all these issues the Court of Justice is the theoretical apex of the legal system. In practice reference to the Court on points of European law may be made by national courts operating below the highest level. Thus in the UK, European reference would be made by the Court of Appeal rather than the House of Lords. At least theoretically, this still leaves room for clashes of jurisdiction.

Reference is often made to the quasi-federal nature of the community, and this may be a good point at which to conclude this basic description of the working of the institutions. Some of the characteristics of federalism were discussed in Chapter 2. Normally there is a considerable degree of autonomy for each level of institutions. In so far as this is not the case with the Community, use of the term 'quasi' may be appropriate. The central institutions have their reserved sphere of activity, with the critical right to pass binding legislation and, as will be shown later, their own source of budget revenue. These are unmistakably federal features. However, national institutions impinge on the Community in a number of ways which are incompatible with a fully federal system. In so far as it is the member states, and not the Council, which appoint the members of both Commission and Court of Justice, neither has full institutional autonomy. Although the Council operates at European level, its participants are still largely creatures of the national or lower dimension. It is the interaction of all these features which have led so many to use the phrase 'sui generis' in describing the Community – 'one of a kind of which there is only one'!

5   The Six in search of an identity

Earlier chapters have shown the extent to which the process of European integration was shaped by context. At the end of the 1950s there was a subtle change in the contours of this context. Until then it had mostly revolved around Europe's position in the world and the impact on the continent of super-power politics. After 1958 an increasingly important part of the context for European integration relates to national political considerations. As Europe's political and institutional system has evolved, so there has been a two-way interaction between it and the political and administrative systems of the member states. In terms of national politics, this involves more than simply taking sides on specific issues concerned with integration. However, in the very early years European integration was only one very small factor in the ebb and flow of national politics. It could be argued that Europe contributed to the downfall of the one effective government in the history of the Fourth Republic – that of Mendès-France in 1955.[1] However, it is stretching credulity to link its fall directly to the collapse of the French Fourth Republic and the return to power of General de Gaulle three years later.

In retrospect, the Fourth Republic, which lasted a mere twelve years, until 1958, had some substantial achievements. It took France into the Community and laid the foundations for the historic reconciliation with Germany. In so doing, it at last cut that umbilical cord which had for so long largely subordinated French initiatives in Europe to British policy. At home the Fourth Republic facilitated (partly through government inertia) the transformation of the French economy based on a series of five-year plans, carried out largely by administrative fiat. The core political problem was that under the constitution none of the central institutions possessed any real authority. An intensely fractured party system and the existence of groups on both right and left which challenged the legitimacy of the entire regime led to a series of governments which could only survive by doing nothing – what the French called '*immobilisme*'. There is an interesting parallel with the Italian system, which had many of the same problems but was able to carry on for three decades longer than its French equivalent. Partly this was because Italy had a dominant political party. However, it was also partly because Italy did not have to face the enormous problem of dismantling a world-wide empire.

By 1958 France was well on the way to divesting itself of its formal imperial role.[2] One problem was unresolved: formally, Algeria was a part of France, but only 10 per cent of its population was ethnically French. Facing a war of national liberation, Paris also had to contend with French settlers opposed to independence. These twin pressures resulted in the fall of governments and ultimately of the regime itself, but there was a bizarre twist. The ongoing war against Arabs in Algeria was one motive for French involvement in Suez. As has been shown, the failure of this adventure was a key factor in French adhesion to the EEC. Shortly thereafter, riots by French settlers, supported by the French army in what amounted to a rebellion, caused the final collapse of the Fourth Republic and the return to power of de Gaulle, who had opposed both the Coal and Steel and the Defence Communities. His record and political platform alike suggested fundamental antagonism towards Community Europe.

It is worth devoting some space to these events, because they are crucial to understanding the series of problems which the communities faced in the 1960s. De Gaulle had resigned as French Prime Minister in 1946 because he was unwilling to accept the constraints on executive power inherent in the constitution then being drafted. The political party he subsequently created was fervently nationalist and opposed to the communities. On the other hand, de Gaulle was himself a believer in Europe, based admittedly on what he felt were the only underlying realities – states and peoples.[3] This was not dissimilar to the British position. However, the overall motivation was quite different. Britain recognised the need for Europeans to work together through co-operation in the context of the Western alliance with the USA. De Gaulle believed that France should seek to create a strong Europe which could resist US pressure. For this reason the Suez fiasco could only reinforce de Gaulle's basically pro-European views.

Before examining events of the 1960s, it is worth emphasising the key role of France in moves towards European integration. Without Franco-German reconciliation, no European entity of any kind was possible. Politically, the lead had to come from France in so far as Germany was still regaining respectability and acceptability after the

Nazi period. In addition, British opposition to European integration meant that Italy and Benelux increasingly looked to France for leadership. During the 1950s the pace of integration had, therefore, been largely determined by what was acceptable to France: by 1958 France was central to the integration process. De Gaulle's dominant motivation when he returned to power at the age of 68 was to restore France to what he considered its rightful position in the world. At home, that meant vesting authority in a powerful executive. In Europe, it necessitated French leadership. The European Community and Britain's voluntary exclusion gave de Gaulle his opportunity. It hardly needs stating that the notion of Europe uniting under French leadership was hardly compatible with the kind of integration advocated by Monnet. In addition, de Gaulle never exhibited any enthusiasm for the actual institutions of Community.[4]

In the pantheon of European heroes and villains de Gaulle is frequently condemned for rejecting supra-nationalism and the nascent 'Community method'. At the time, de Gaulle seemed to embody a resurgence of nationalism – a counter-pose to Jean Monnet and integration.[5] Thirty years on, perspectives are perhaps slightly different. It is a central part of the thesis of this book that the well-springs of integration sprang from very clear perceptions of national interest on the part of a group of European countries. In this respect de Gaulle's view of French national interest was clearly different. However, he was the first national statesman to appreciate the extent to which the nascent communities themselves offered a battlefield on which national interests could be effectively pursued. For a period of ten years de Gaulle and France used the Community to espouse those interests and in effect to take on both Britain and the supporters of integration/supra-nationalism/federalism.

The first clear indication of the new French approach arose out of negotiations for another now long-forgotten European initiative. Although rejecting membership of the EEC, Britain was concerned about the economic implications of being left outside. Accordingly, in 1956 Britain put forward a proposal for a European Free Trade Area covering the whole of the OEEC. It would promote free trade in industrial products between its members, including the EEC, but there would be no common tariff, no joint economic and social policies and no long-term political aspirations. Such an arrangement would not disrupt traditional trade between Britain and the Commonwealth. Negotiations continued for two years. The Six, anxious to prevent the Community from being weakened by simultaneous participation in a looser arrangement, showed little enthusiasm. France was hostile, claiming it would offer few of the advantages of the Community whilst intensifying France's own economic problems. French tariffs were relatively high to protect its own industry. Under EEC rules they would disappear for internal Community trade; in addition the common external tariff, which would apply to imports from non-member countries, would also be lower. The Free Trade Area would have meant yet more competition for French industry. However, under the near moribund French Fourth Republic, no clear governmental decision emerged. All this changed when de Gaulle took over as Prime Minister: within six months France in effect took unilateral action to end the negotiations. It was a harbinger of Gaullist methods, but on this occasion evoked little condemnation within the Community.

The outcome posed a major dilemma for Britain. Past policy had been based on assumptions that an economic community was both undesirable in theory and unlikely to be achieved in practice. There had also been a tendency to exaggerate the strength of Britain's bargaining position. The Six had gone ahead and signed the Treaty of Paris, but the collapse of the EDC and its replacement by the Western European Union suggested that Britain was still a major player in Europe. British policy had been predicated on an assumption that, in the unlikely event of the EEC being established, it would be possible to find an arrangement to avoid total British exclusion. Although signature of the Rome treaties and ending of the free trade negotiations exposed the underlying weakness of this strategy, the lesson did not seem to have been learned. Britain's response was to join with Sweden in promoting a European Free Trade Association (EFTA) of seven countries outside the Community,[6] in the hope that this would precipitate a more general arrangement between the two groupings. However, the Community refused to participate in any multilateral negotiations. Britain had to face the reality that only full membership of the Community could prevent exclusion from its economic benefits and in July 1961 made a formal application to join. Similar applications were also made by Denmark, Ireland and Norway.

The negotiations which followed ran until January 1963. Formally, their scope was vast, since Britain was seeking a variety of special arrangements for members of the Commonwealth, both industrialised and developing, and also for its existing partners in EFTA.[7] Yet somehow the critical dialogue on the future orientation of British policy and the willingness of existing members to assist a 'convert' never took place. In part this was because Britain was clearly in a weak bargaining position precisely because it was operating from the outside and negotiating for so many not always compatible interests. The reverse of the coin is that, whereas the entry of Britain would clearly be contrary to the new French aspirations, de Gaulle was himself not in practice strong enough simply to give an immediate 'no'. The difficulty was that he had not yet resolved the Algerian conundrum which had brought him back to power. Until he did so, he was dependent on support from the old parties of the Fourth Republic, amongst whom there was considerable support for British entry. In addition, the other five were much more favourable to British membership than they had been to the free trade proposal. In the circumstances, all the French negotiators could do was bargain toughly and temporise. In this they had a powerful, if unwitting, ally in Britain's failure to realise that time was not on its side. Britain was seeking to sort out all the details, potentially involving a large proportion of world trade, as a precondition for a decision to join. In a welter of detail, the British government never sought to check out the real terms and the real price for entry. The strategic and tactical failures were complete.

Had the negotiations reached a conclusion before summer 1962, it is conceivable that de Gaulle would have had to accept British membership. However, by the end of the year there was a major change in the French political scene. In the summer, de Gaulle resolved the Algerian problem by agreeing to independence, a move ratified by referendum. He and the old political parties had no further need of each other and in November 1962 de Gaulle's Union pour la Nouvelle République gained a massive electoral triumph. The President at last had the domestic base which gave him the space to pursue his foreign policy goals, and in January 1963 he used the vehicle of a press conference to announce the effective end of enlargement negotiations.

Diplomatic historians continue to argue about motivations for the French veto. Much attention has focused on the December 1962 Nassau agreement, by which the USA agreed to supply Britain with the Polaris missiles essential for delivery of its 'independent' nuclear deterrent. Clearly, de Gaulle found the agreement objectionable and a proof that Britain was too closely linked to the USA. However, that had always been his view and Nassau did no more than confirm it. We may fantasise as to de Gaulle's reaction had Britain offered to join France in establishing a joint nuclear deterrent as an alternative to reliance on the USA. This possibility was never remotely feasible. In fact, Nassau was not the reason for the veto. However, it did offer the opportunity, for it enabled de Gaulle to proclaim that Britain, unlike France, was not really 'European'. The reality is that de Gaulle saw Britain inside the Community as a rival for leadership, and that was sufficient reason for a veto once he had the political strength.

From a British perspective there is a temptation to suggest that France's veto was another defining moment in post-war Europe. This is both over-simplistic and misleading. Later in the decade, Britain under a Labour government made a further application for negotiations to joint the Community. France expressed renewed opposition and the application simply remained on the table. After the resignation of de Gaulle and the defeat of the Labour government, it was to form the basis for successful negotiations and Britain's accession in 1973. In this sense de Gaulle merely delayed what may be considered inevitable. Ten years on, the choices for Britain were starker, but in many ways it remained a 'reluctant European'. It seems unlikely that earlier British membership would in practice have made very much difference to the overall direction of Community development, although the detail of policy might have varied.

Just eight days after the veto, France and Germany signed their historic Treaty of Friendship. At a trivial level it might appear that de Gaulle was mocking both Britain and supporters of its entry. However, there can be no doubt as to the deep symbolism of this event. Formally and publicly it sought to lay to rest centuries of hostility between German states and France. After three wars in seventy-five years, the treaty removed armed conflict as a means of settling disputes between two historic enemies. In reality, the treaty was not a stand-alone event: reconciliation between France and Germany was both a necessary condition for, and a prime objective of, the establishment of the communities. However, there are two other facets of this new treaty. First, it reflected important but failed discussion within the Community about the issue of political union. Second – and this would be a kind of defining moment for the Community – it firmly established the concept of a Franco-German axis already discussed in Chapter 3. Henceforth the relationship between France and Germany would be crucial in determining the pace, scope and extent of European integration. These related factors are worth discussion in a little more detail.

In the now nearly fifty-year history of the Community, political union has often seemed to be the 'ghost at the feast'. Earlier chapters have shown the importance of political motives in the establishment of the different communities. It is quite explicit in the preamble to the ECSC treaty that the goal is some form of political unity. However, the early successes of the Six and the Community were primarily economic. The first specific attempt to move directly into the political sphere collapsed with rejection of the EDC. By early 1961 member states were willing to try again, and to this end they established an inter-governmental committee on Political Union.[8] Initial proposals by the French government were very much in line with de Gaulle's thinking. There would be a Union of States directed by a quarterly Council meeting at Heads of State level, with Foreign Ministers meeting in the intervening periods. Decisions would be taken unanimously. Preparation would be in the hands of a new Political Commission composed of senior officials from national ministries and based in Paris.

Years later, many of these French ideas were to be incorporated into the Political Co-operation machinery, but the position in 1961 was different. Within the Community supra-nationalism was still the dominant approach to European unity. There were fears that the supra-national communities might in effect be dissolved into a much looser union. Another issue concerned the parallel enlargement negotiations. Belgium and the Netherlands feared that France wanted to wrap up the negotiations prior to British entry or even use the new Union as a means of keeping Britain out of the Community. A highly complex diplomatic game ensued, although the exact linkage between enlargement and progress towards a Political Union was highly obscure. Objections to the French scheme were held most strongly by those who were also most supportive of British entry. However, the enlargement negotiations were about membership of the Economic Community as established by the Treaty of Rome. Britain had never even contemplated parallel political developments, and it would certainly have rejected out of hand an extension of the supra-national method to the political realm.

Attempts were made to formulate a joint response to French proposals by the other five and to set out an alternative vision of Political Union. The Dutch were in the vanguard, supporting twin, albeit possibly contradictory, goals of enlargement and supra-national political organs. Although they gained some support from Belgium and Italy, de Gaulle countered this through a series of bilateral discussions with German Chancellor Adenauer. By mid 1962 negotiations for Political Union had effectively run out of steam, but the French concept resurfaced in the Franco-German treaty. The two Heads of Government would meet quarterly to plan their co-operation, which would be implemented by foreign ministers. Officials would meet regularly, as would defence ministers. The governments also agreed to consult before taking decisions on issues of foreign policy.

The mechanics were to turn out to be far less important than the spirit, although, hardly surprisingly, they evoked a considerable outcry within the Community coming so soon after the veto on enlargement.

Taken literally, the new treaty suggested that France and Germany might hold advance bilateral discussions on key issues confronting the Community, thus giving it in effect a two-country directorate. In practice, this is to read too much into a text which was stronger on rhetoric than practicalities. However, France and Germany had established an informal 'axis', which would be critical to Community development. From de Gaulle's perspective, France was lending Germany respectability and accepting its economic dominance, but in exchange France was gaining the political leadership central to his world perspective. The immediate impact of the Franco-German alignment was significantly softened by the resignation of Adenauer before the end of 1963. If the basic understanding between France and Germany persisted, relations between their Heads of Government at a personal level were never to be quite so warm until the very different leadership of Giscard and Schmidt in the mid 1970s.

There is a sense in which the Franco-German treaty did no more than point in sharp relief to one simple underlying reality. This reality was that the Community could rarely proceed when France and Germany were in fundamental disagreement. De Gaulle exploited this quite ruthlessly through his considerable strategic skill and willingness to go to the brink. After the veto, there was talk in Britain of the 'friendly five' and the possibility of a diplomatic move which would enable negotiations to continue. The Franco-German alignment put paid to that hope.

At first sight all these developments – the French veto on enlargement, the failed negotiations for Political Union, the Franco-German treaty – are purely European events, but it is still appropriate to relate them to the wider international context and specifically to the Cold War. There had been occasions during the 1950s when armed conflict between East and West had seemed possible. The argument in Chapter 2 is that during the 1960s the Cold War ossified. A key stage in this process was the construction of the Berlin Wall in 1961. At one level this was the Soviet response to the constant haemorrhage of peoples going West, but at another level it represented a final, and seemingly irrevocable, separation of two worlds. The USSR had been sending a clear message by the way in which they handled dissent in Eastern Europe, especially the events in Hungary in 1956 – 'what we have, we hold'. The message was reinforced by the Berlin Wall. However, at a psychological level the wall also suggested that the USSR had no designs further West. It follows that the concept of two Germanies and two Europes with definitive frontiers was now apparently immutable. Once the implications had been assessed a future German Social

Democrat government would be free to practise what it called 'Ostpolitik'. This was based on recognition of the reality of two Germanies, and it was a means of seeking to normalise relations with the German Democratic Republic. Because Ostpolitik did not challenge the existence of the frontier, it in no way countered the basic commitment of the Federal Republic to European integration or of the Democratic Republic's position in the Communist world. It is also significant that throughout the international crisis occasioned by the construction of the wall, de Gaulle was unequivocal in his support for the Federal Republic. Whatever the Soviet intentions, the construction of the wall effectively sealed the Federal Republic into Western Europe and in effect into the Community. It further underpinned the Franco-German alignment.

It was tempting to refer in the title of this chapter to doubts and divisions, and at first sight this may seem to characterise the Community and its problems in the 1960s. There were indeed a series of apparent internal crises, and at the time they seemed to suggest that the Community was in some danger. However, its existence was never really threatened. The reality was that the major political decisions to create and sustain the Community had been made. They reflected and were reinforced by the external world. Within the Community de Gaulle was the instrumental figure as these events unfolded. His preoccupation was with broad policy issues – '*grandes lignes*' is the evocative French phrase. De Gaulle wanted to assert French leadership in the Community, hence his rejection of Britain; and he sought a Union of States rather than a fully integrated or federated Europe. These were the twin issues which actually provoked the crises and created considerable friction between France and several of its partners, especially the Netherlands. However, it is important not to give a misleading impression of how the Community actually operated and developed in the 1960s.

The key point is that there was no difference between France and its partners as to the centrality of Europe in their national policies. Precisely because de Gaulle had a limited interest in, and knowledge of, economics, he was reasonably supportive of regular Community activity. The EEC Treaty had laid down a precise timetable for attaining a customs union for industrial products, and France was willing to facilitate this on one condition. This concerned the establishment of a common agricultural policy (CAP), the financing of which would be based on producer rather than consumer interests. The potential linkage between industrial customs union and agriculture was a fecund area for the Franco-German axis. With the help of the

Commission, which was developing the concept of the package, a deal could be struck: the CAP was established with appropriate financial structures, and implementation of the customs union actually accelerated, so that it would be fully operational by July 1968.

There was no sense in which such a 'great leap forward' could be self-contained. Internally it raised issues concerned with Community resources and the role of the institutions. However, decisions on issues concerned with the external tariff and agricultural policies were bound to impact on the Community's external relations. By the mid 1960s the Community was already a major player in world trade discussions. Its own policies were now helping to determine the external context. This was to be another ingredient of the next major internal Community crisis in the 1960s. The USA supported integration as a means of strengthening Western Europe, but did not want to pay too high an economic price in lost trade. This was the background to various international trade talks through the aegis of the General Agreement on Tariffs and Trade (GATT). By the mid 1960s the Commission was planning the Community's bargaining position for the impending Kennedy round of tariff negotiations. This raised particular problems for France, which had traditionally been much more protectionist than Germany.

Before examining the crisis which resulted from interaction of these issues, it is worth making the point that in the early 1960s the supranational Commission saw itself as an essential and independent political driving force behind the Community and integration. In addition, the need to agree the CAP had led to very close relations between the Commission and French officials. This helps explain the presentation by the Commission during 1964 and the early part of 1965 of a proposed package deal which appeared to link completion of the CAP with a variety of financial and institutional issues and with the establishment of a mandate for participation in the Kennedy round. De Gaulle's reaction was that France was in effect being asked to pay twice for agreement on the CAP, and, crucially, that the Commission was exceeding its role.

The actual occasion for the 1965/66 institutional crisis had much less impact on the Community than its consequences.[9] De Gaulle's immediate objectives were to re-assert French primacy in the Community and to promote his concept of a Union of States. Two institutional issues surfaced: one concerned the independent political role of the Commission, whilst the other related to the use of majority voting in the Council. The French view was that the Commission should in effect be under the control of the Council and its members,

and operating within defined mandates. Council decisions would
normally be reached by unanimity. The latter ran against the spirit and
even the letter of the EEC Treaty, under which qualified majority
voting would be progressively introduced.

Throughout the second half of 1965 France simply boycotted the
institutions. Although existing commitments continued to be implemented, further integration was clearly impossible. The crisis was only
resolved following a ministerial meeting in Luxembourg in January
1966. The statement then produced by ministers has been variously
described as the 'Luxembourg agreement' or 'Luxembourg compromise'. For years thereafter the document was cited as justification for
claiming the right to exercise a national veto over Community decision
making. That was in accordance with the French view as then
expressed, but the other five did not agree, as the crucial section of the
ministerial text makes clear:[10]

> Where, in the case of decisions which may be taken by majority vote
> on a proposal of the Commission, very important interests of one
> or more partners are at stake, the Members of the Community will
> endeavour, within a reasonable time, to reach solutions which can
> be adopted by all the Members of the Council ... the French dele-
> gation considers that where very important interests are at stake the
> discussion must be continued until unanimous agreement is
> reached. The six delegations note that there is a divergence of views
> on what should be done in the event of a failure to reach complete
> agreement. The six delegations nevertheless consider that this diver-
> gence does not prevent the Community's work being resumed in
> accordance with the normal procedure.

The only agreement or compromise is that the Six would continue
with the work of integration despite a major and unresolved disagreement on an important constitutional issue. For, so long as de Gaulle
remained at the helm, France would claim the right of veto, whatever
the treaty provisions. A major Community player had apparently
demonstrated a willingness to jeopardise the whole Community in
defence of its position, or at the very least had displayed better
brinkmanship. However, once de Gaulle ceased to be President of
France, the Luxembourg statement gradually became little more than
another constitutional reference point when members disagreed. Later
on, after the Community was enlarged, it was Britain which most
frequently cited the French view on majority rule in support of a
variety of idiosyncratic positions. At no time did the so-called
'Luxembourg compromise' have any real constitutional force, but as a

reference point in controversy it did not disappear until the Single European Act of 1986.[11]

President de Gaulle was the dominant figure in the Community during the 1960s. It is all too easy for proponents of integration to dismiss him as a 'man of the day before yesterday', holding up supposedly inevitable progress towards a Europe united on supra-national lines. In fact, the notion that de Gaulle reintroduced nationalism into post-war Western Europe is superficial on all counts. The Europe of the 1960s already differed from that of the late 1940s when the concepts of integration and unification were being developed. The Cold War had now ossified within set boundaries. In 1956 the brutal suppression of the Hungarian rising was cited – possibly erroneously – as proof that the expansionist ambitions of the USSR remained. Twelve years later the ending of the attempts to present Communism with a 'human face' in Prague was just one more indication of the apparent permanence of the Iron Curtain as a two-way security boundary.

By the mid 1960s, the states of Western Europe could feel more secure and more confident. The immediate military threat had eased, their political stability was assured and economic growth seemed permanent. In the evocative words of Alan Milward, Europe had indeed rescued the nation state. In this context it seems hardly likely that there would have been – even in the absence of de Gaulle – a smooth transition to a united, supra-national Europe. In the light of subsequent events it hardly, for example, seems likely that earlier British membership would have strengthened the pro-integration forces within the Community! The underlying reality was that, as nation states recovered their strength and nerve, they would again be key actors in the evolution of Europe. This was the essential lesson to be drawn from de Gaulle's apparently idiosyncratic behaviour. The future of the Community would depend on an accommodation between the interplay of national interests and the process of integration. The reality is that, by focusing on this key point, de Gaulle actually made a positive contribution to the development of unification.

6   Widening and deepening

The beginning of the 1970s witnessed a changing of the guard in Western Europe. De Gaulle, his internal work of reconstruction completed, resigned in 1969 after losing a referendum. His replacement, Pompidou, seemed far more in keeping with the spirit of the times. Later the same year Brandt became German Chancellor and in 1970 Heath became British Prime Minister. From a European point of view the changes seemed to bode well. It had been easy enough for the integrationists to lay the blame for the problems of the sixties entirely at the door of President de Gaulle. Although Pompidou was a Gaullist, it seemed highly unlikely that he would be able to assert French national interests in quite the same way. In Germany, there was a smooth transition to a government led for the first time by a Social Democrat, who already enjoyed an immense reputation. In Britain, the return of a Conservative government suggested a much more positive attitude towards Europe. Although Prime Minister Wilson had lodged Britain's second application to join the Community, the Labour Party was deeply divided on the issue. Heath, who had led the negotiations for entry in 1961–63, was by contrast strongly pro-British entry and seemed in full control of his party.

The European heritage of these new leaders was, despite the problems and crises of the sixties, considerable. The customs union had been established according to the accelerated timetable; the common agricultural policy (CAP) was in place; institutions of the three communities had been merged in 1967; the Community had been a key actor in the successful Kennedy round of world trade negotiations and had also established bilateral trading arrangements with large numbers of third countries. In late 1969 the six Heads of Government met at a summit conference in the Hague. Hitherto such meetings had been spasmodic and were seen as a 'dignified' addition to the panoply of institutions. However, circumstances pointed to a need for a fresh injection of political will into the process of integration: decisions to bring this about could only come from Heads of Government. If nothing else, the sixties had proved conclusively that the process would not continue indefinitely and automatically. 'Spill-over'[1] would not of itself lead to a united Europe.

Assessment of the period ushered in by the Hague summit up to the signature of the Single European Act sixteen years later is controversial. It was commonplace during the time to bemoan the apparent lack of substantive progress, particularly in economic and monetary union, and above all, failure to reform the institutions. Retrospectively the judgement must be a little different. What happened during those years was a gradual confirmation of two verdicts. One was that integration would continue and that a growing number of West European states would act collectively in an increasing number of spheres. On this basis the integrationists could consider de Gaulle as no more than a footnote to history. However, there is another verdict which subtly merges the legacies of Monnet and de Gaulle. The sectoral approach would continue – involving as appropriate both integration and inter-governmental co-operation. However, there would be no rapid move to a European federation. The conclusion is that during this period above all, the Community can only be judged on its own terms: for what it was actually undertaking and for how well it was performing, and not for any subsequent evolution it might inspire.

Earlier chapters have demonstrated how the integration process and the Community were conditioned by the external environment. During the sixties the Community itself became a part of both the European polity and the accepted international structure. Although many contemporary analysts were slow to recognise it, the Community was by the end of the 1960s a part of the normal, regular international world. Internally its members operated in precisely the same way as they did in any international arena, seeking what they deemed the most effective ways in which to further their particular national interests. Externally the Community had become a major international actor which reinforced the strength and standing of those same members. This was also the time when the Community's recent treaty-based origins had clearly become less important as a means of understanding how it actually operated. Custom and practice were developed side by side with law. Analysts needed to focus on behaviour as well as structure and functions. Not infrequently, obsession with legal technicalities obfuscated the fact that the Community operated, like most organisations, in accordance with 'rules of the game'.

Crucial to an understanding of this period is a recognition of the importance of bargaining within the Council of Ministers and, at the highest level, at summit meetings, subsequently renamed the European Council. It is in this sense that the so-called Luxembourg compromise, discussed in Chapter 5, is so unhelpful as a key to understanding how the Community actually worked. The Council may have most of the legislative powers, but it does not operate like a normal legislature. Its dominant characteristic is that of a bargaining forum where member states assert their different interests, which have to be accommodated in a process of power broking. The first power broker was the Commission, fulfilling one of its functions of seeking to harmonise the differing views and interests of member states. Increasingly important as a second power broker was the Council Presidency. Package agreements were assembled which linked disparate problems, but, by offering something to everybody, facilitated agreement and ensured progress.

The agreements reached at the Hague summit are a benchmark of this approach. Applications for membership were on the table from Britain, Denmark, Ireland and Norway. These had long since received generalised support from five member states, but this was now reinforced by the more pro-active policy of Willie Brandt, the new German Chancellor. His major foreign policy initiative was to be a new Ostpolitik. This was clearly based on acceptance of two German states and, therefore, of the Iron Curtain. If anything, Brandt was reinforcing the commitment of the Federal Republic to the integration process. However, this was not necessarily the view at the time, and least of all in Paris. There is a good deal of evidence to suggest that Pompidou was worried by increasing German economic weight in the Community and anxious about the political implications of Ostpolitik.[2] It may be over-stating the argument to suggest a reversion in French thinking to the position in the mid-1950s, but Britain could conceivably offer a counter-weight to Germany. Pompidou's domestic position was also slightly different from that of his predecessor, in that he had a clearer need of support from the moderate largely pro-European centre right. Indeed, without the support of Giscard's Independent Republicans, Pompidou would not have been elected President.

The French had an additional motivation at the Hague. Although the CAP had been firmly established earlier in the 1960s, there was a clear French national interest in finalising the financial arrangements before British entry. This could only be in the context of the Community acquiring its own budget, with some control ultimately being exercised by the European Parliament. This offered a major concession to the integrationists, who were particularly strong in the governments of Italy and the Benelux. Such an arrangement would have been anathema to de Gaulle: in the new context it seemed a logical way forward.

The outcome of the Hague summit was described by President Pompidou in terms of a triptych of completion, development and enlargement. In the first category were financial arrangements for the agricultural policy and agreement on making available to the Community its 'own' resources. The second involved a commitment to consider proposals for political co-operation and an even looser suggestion concerning possible economic and monetary union. The third, which would follow the first and parallel the second, committed all members to British entry.

The twelve months which followed the Hague meeting rekindled the 1969 already 'rose-tinted' view of a so-called golden age of integration – the early period when the communities were being established – and almost seemed to justify the Heads of Government in claiming that 'today the Community has arrived at a turning point in its history'. In April 1970 the Six finally agreed on new budgetary provisions based on the Community having its 'own resources'. These would be the proceeds of the common external tariff, agricultural levies and a uniform VAT rate not to exceed 1 per cent. Given the elaboration of common policies to date, the bulk of expenditure from that budget would undoubtedly be on agriculture. The financial regime was reinforced by a further treaty in 1975, which introduced new institutional arrangements and in particular granted significant powers over the budget to the European Parliament, which became for the first time a major player in decision making.

Pompidou thus succeeded in his twin goals of completing the edifice of the CAP and establishing a new financial regime prior to British entry. In so far as these financial arrangements were extremely favourable for France this was a major tactical victory. However, it was to store up endless trouble for the entire Community, since the arrangements were for technical reasons highly unfavourable to Britain. A series of special rebates, arrangements and exemptions were made until 1984, when the Fontainebleau agreement formalised a special system for Britain which will last until at least 1999. The 'own resources' system should have been fully operational by 1975, but in effect it has never been fully implemented.[3]

The long-delayed second set of enlargement negotiations finally opened at the end of June 1970. They were formally in response to Britain's application made more than three years previously by the then Labour government, led by Harold Wilson. However, the British general election a few weeks before the negotiations opened brought the Conservatives back to office. Edward Heath was certainly the most pro-European and pro-Community of any post-war British prime minister. In the last analysis this ensured British entry but at a price: Labour in opposition increasingly adopted the same critical posture as in 1961 at the time of the first negotiations.

Essentially, the success of these second negotiations was ensured by another of the increasingly rare moments of harmony between governments in London and Paris. As was the case a decade earlier, the ebb and flow of detailed negotiations told only part of the story. This time, however, it was French negotiators 'on the ground' who were in a sense 'wrong footed' by an extraneous political decision in Paris. In fact the negotiations concentrated on a small number of 'key' issues – the trade position of New Zealand, butter, sugar, financial regulations and, in the later stages, the fisheries regulation. As before, French officials played a major role in the negotiations and very little progress was made for almost a year. However, towards the end of May 1971 a political decision was taken in Paris – but this time to facilitate British entry. Earlier that month, Germany had 'floated' the mark, almost certainly against French advice, and there had been a successful meeting (of minds) in Paris between Pompidou and Heath. The die was cast and the first enlargement treaty was signed in January 1972. British accession was ratified in the House of Commons but only with some cross-party voting to ensure majority support. The other three applicants held referendums which resulted in Denmark and Ireland joining and Norway withdrawing its application.

At the time, a good deal of attention was focused on what were called the 'terms' of membership. However, much of the debate which took place in Britain on the so-called 'terms' was essentially phoney. The real issue was whether or not Britain should finally join in the process of European integration, which would necessitate British acceptance of the 'Community method' and the 'acquis communautaire'.[4] In essence, Britain was now accepting an approach which had been immediately and automatically rejected previously. None of the so-called 'key' issues was definitively resolved in the negotiations. In effect, the three newcomers were accepting the 'Community method' of 'agreeing to agree'. The nine (six former and three new) members signed up for the enlarged Community, established a number of transitional arrangements, adjusted institutional provisions and, through a variety of different verbal formulations, agreed to resolve the major issues in due course. From most points of view the newcomers remained at a disadvantage compared to what would have been the case had they joined in the beginning. Outside or inside, their ability to change or roll back two decades of integration was bound to be limited. In practice, also, the shared political will which characterised and facilitated issue resolution in the early years of the Community was never present to the same degree in the 1970s. As a result, arguments over issues which it had been agreed to resolve dragged on almost interminably. When Labour returned to power, Harold Wilson sought to renegotiate the 'terms' in a bid to reconcile the party to Europe. Apart from extending the special financial arrangements for Britain, the re-negotiation had little impact on the operation of the Community. However, it did resolve Harold Wilson's major political problem. There was a large majority for continued membership at the first referendum ever held nation-wide. The result was a belated popular approval of British membership and, in effect, a fresh endorsement of the Wilson government. The terms as such were hardly an issue, since they were both incomprehensible to the general public and almost totally irrelevant to the real debate. As already mentioned, arguments over the budget continued – in an increasingly ill-tempered manner – until 1984. Controversy over fishing regulations has for a variety of reasons carried on for even longer.

Another major achievement of 1970 was agreement to begin European Political Co-operation (EPC). Aspirations to transform the basis of Europe's foreign relations had been present since the beginning of the integration process. This was a significant feature of the abortive discussions on Political Union held during the early 1960s and discussed in the previous chapter. The new initiative was based on what was to become known as the Luxembourg report, and it established procedures for consultation with a view to co-operation on issues of foreign policy. This would take place outside the formal Community framework with only minimal involvement of Commission and Parliament. Ministerial meetings were to be held twice a year. Formally separate from the Council of Ministers, they would take place in the capital of the country holding the Presidency. National officials would prepare for the meetings. In most respects these arrangements were less far reaching than those proposed by France during the previous negotiations and rejected then as insufficiently integrationist by the other member states.

Given this low-key beginning, it is hardly surprising that EPC developed slowly, only acquiring a treaty base with the Single European Act in the mid 1980s. As early as 1973 provision was made for four ministerial meetings a year and improved liaison with

Community institutions. That same year extraneous factors virtually shipwrecked the nascent structure, although they also strengthened perceptions as to the centrality of Europe's need for political co-operation. The Middle East war divided Europe's sympathies, but demonstrated shared dependence on (mostly imported) oil. For a time, dialogue with Arab oil producers was a major concern of EPC. If the nine did not exactly cover themselves with glory during this process, they were none the less being helped yet again by the external world to forge a corporate identity – this time in the political realm. The other major substantive activity of EPC involved preparation of common positions for the Conference on Security and Co-operation in Europe. A balance sheet of the real achievements of the Conference must perforce lie outside the scope of this book, but in terms of co-ordinated policy preparation and presentation it was a considerable success for the EPC.[5]

Another commitment made at the Hague concerned Economic and Monetary Union (EMU). This was perhaps the first official mention of what was to become another long-term aspiration for the Community. The central concerns of the EEC are the creation of a customs union and the development of a range of common economic policies. EMU could be seen as the logical culmination of inter-related processes of economic and monetary integration. One would be a gradual progress of economic convergence involving successive phases of co-ordination, harmonisation and, ultimately, a unified economic policy; whilst the other would involve the locking of exchange rates and ultimately a single currency. Following a report by Pierre Werner, Prime Minister of Luxembourg, the member states agreed on a phased approach to monetary union. Initially, exchange rates between the European currencies would be fixed within narrow bands. Thus linked together, they would 'float' against other world currencies, particularly the dollar. The arrangement became known as the 'snake in the tunnel'.

In contrast to the ongoing, if very slow, progress in the political field, this early attempt at monetary union was to be one of the Community's more spectacular failures. The intention was that the snake in the tunnel, accompanied by substantial measures of economic co-ordination, would pave the way for a single currency. Even if the political will had been present for such a leap forward – and the reality was a complete absence of basic agreement between Britain, France and Germany – there would have been enormous problems. The post-war exchange arrangement, Bretton Woods, which fixed the value of all currencies against a dollar convertible into gold, was gradually unfolding. The world had become dependent on massive external US expenditure, which meant increasing US debts. As these mounted, the role of the US as world banker became ever less credible. Speculation and international movements of 'hot' money placed enormous pressure on all exchange rates, including those of the Community member states. In the circumstances, maintenance of relatively stable intra-Community exchange rates became impossible. In addition, the long post-war boom effectively came to an end with the explosion in oil prices consequent on the Middle East war. Following the Werner report, the commitments in respect of economic convergence, as distinct from the arrangements for the snake in the tunnel, were exceedingly vague. In practice, given the international economic problems of the 1970s, economic convergence was hardly likely to be a major priority for member states.

Debates in the 1970s were often a precursor to those of the 1990s. Three concepts have seemingly been ever present in discussions about the future direction of the Community – political co-operation, economic and monetary union and European union. Two of these have already been discussed, and in both cases developments in the process were largely determined by changes in the external context. Once started, political co-operation evolved slowly but relatively consistently in response to external stimuli. The need for economic and monetary union was seemingly reinforced by chaos in world money markets, but for some years the same factor made progress virtually impossible. The third of this triptych – and potentially the most far-reaching – was European Union. In October 1972 the Paris summit formally adopted 'the major objective of transforming, before the end of the decade and with the fullest respect for the Treaties already signed, the whole complex of the relations of Member States into a European Union'. There was little indication of what this would mean and no mechanics for implementation. Two years later there was another summit in Paris – with further changes in the 'dramatis personae' or cast list! Giscard, a non-Gaullist conservative, was now President of France, whilst Wilson was again British Prime Minister. Schmidt succeeded Brandt as German Chancellor, leading the same coalition of Social Democrats and Free Democrats. The Paris summit asked the Belgian Prime Minister, Leo Tindemanns, to report on European Union. Bizarrely, it was Harold Wilson – whose main concern at the time was re-negotiation – who persuaded Giscard that Tindemanns was the 'man for the job'. The Heads of Government also agreed that in future they would formalise their meetings as the European Council and as such take an over-view of

Community, Political Co-operation and any other activities. Finally, it was determined that the European Parliament would be directly elected from 1979. Each of these decisions had potentially far-reaching implications.

Prior to 1969, summit meetings had been infrequent and, as mentioned above, to some extent they were little more than a dignified addition to the panoply of institutional activity. Long before 1969 it had become apparent that integration would never develop beyond a certain stage, simply on the basis of the shared political will evinced in the 1950s. This alone would be insufficient to transform the basic treaty commitments. Renewal of political will required the participation of national leaders, who alone had the authority to take decisions to extend the range of Community activity. The underlying institutional problem over the five years from the Hague to the second Paris summit arose from the leaders' succcess in restoring some velocity to the Community. In so doing they made themselves indispensable, and effectively circumscribed the capacity of the Council of Ministers to take major decisions. This being the case, even annual summits could not give the required momentum to the integration process. The decision was taken to transform summits into the European Council, which would meet three times a year. The new institution, quite outside the treaty framework, rapidly became a key part of the Community structure. It automatically assumed a critical role in taking major decisions and in resolving conflicts. It also helped bridge the potential divide between Community activity and that undertaken under the aegis of political co-operation. Not until the Single European Act did the European Council receive treaty recognition.[6] 1974-86

Before 1974, proposals for direct elections had been held up by French Gaullist insistence that it would be inappropriate to hold them for a body with so few powers (which they were not prepared to increase!). The first elections took place in June 1979. Transnational linkages between parties were very tenuous, and in effect there were nine separate national contests. In all, around 110 million people voted, turn-out varying from 91 per cent in Belgium (where voting is compulsory) to little more than 32 per cent in Britain. The major political importance of the elections lay in helping to give the Community some kind of human, accountable face. It also eased the way for Parliament to acquire greater powers over Community legislation in the subsequent Single European Act and Maastricht Treaty, and helped promote interest in concepts such as European citizenship.

As exercises in democracy, elections to the European Parliament (there have now been four) have been fraught with problems. Although transnational party links have become stronger, domestic factors have always been the major determinant of results in any one country. Whilst some votes have been cast for specifically, often transient 'anti-European' groupings, most have not been cast on European issues. Turn-out has only increased as a function of Community enlargement. On most statistical tests it actually fell over the first four direct elections. In 1994 it varied from the same 91 per cent in Belgium down to less than 36 per cent in Portugal.[7] In theory, direct elections contribute towards establishing the democratic legitimacy of the Community as a whole. Their existence has been used as a lever to gain more influence for the Parliament over decision making. However, in contrast with the position in member states, the European Parliament is not the basis for Community government and its role in legislation remains heavily circumscribed. Inevitably this affects electoral turn-out.

Earlier in this chapter it was pointed out how often it was argued at the time – and indeed even subsequently – that the Community achieved relatively little between the first enlargement and the signature of the Single European Act. There is a mythology that somehow the Community had lost its way. This chapter has already shown the extent to which this picture is exaggerated. The next chapter will look at some of the later events, but in the 1970s the only years of virtual non-achievement were those between the first enlargement and the elaboration of the European Monetary System. The most obvious features were distraction over the so-called renegotiation of Britain's terms of entry, failure of the Werner plan and the snake in the tunnel, and the fact that European Union was not so much a chimera as a damp squib. There was no tangible result from either the Tindemanns initiative or from a number of other reports about the Community and its institutions.[8] However, part of the reason for the malaise lay in a significant change in the external context. The Middle East war demonstrated the limitations of early arrangements for political co-operation, but it also introduced a severe change in the international economic climate. The enormous increase in oil prices consequent upon the war pushed the Western world into a recession. Until then the Community's historic experience had been of continuous economic growth and increasing prosperity. One immediate implication of this economic change was that, unlike the original Six, Britain's first experience of membership coincided with major economic problems.

A key factor of the mid 1970s was a return to the Franco-German understanding which had characterised earlier developments: once again progress would be a function of their co-operation. After Heath left office, Britain again largely sidelined itself from major influence by concentration first on re-negotiation and subsequently on the issue of budgetary rebates. The power equation persisted into the eighties, when Mitterrand and Kohl again transcended party differences to keep the Franco-German axis central to the Community. Britain's hostile attitude towards increasing integration, together with Thatcher's 'Indian summer' relationship with President Reagan, continued to prevent Britain from claiming any position centre stage.

Agreement between France and Germany was clearly a necessary precondition for establishment of the European Monetary System (EMS) at the end of the 1970s, but of itself it was insufficient. At the beginning of 1977 Roy Jenkins became President of the Commission. A previous Home Secretary and Chancellor of the Exchequer, he remains the most heavyweight former national politician to have held the post. His appointment was occasioned in part by the vagaries of British politics. Vociferously pro-European, his views were always a potential embarrassment to the more pragmatic Wilson and Callaghan who led Labour governments in the seventies. On the other hand, both could see the advantage of a British President, and there was no other contender likely to be acceptable to Giscard and Schmidt.

Jenkins' background put him in a much better position than most of his predecessors to engage national leaders in negotiations as an equal. Given the failure of efforts at Economic and Monetary Union, there was no inevitability about the establishment of EMS. Jenkins' role was decisive, but his own memoirs emphasise the importance of the external context – 'The trigger was the fall of the dollar. In October 1977 . . . a dollar bought 2.30 D-marks. By February 1976 its value was down to DM-2.02 (it went down further to DM 1.76 by that autumn) . . . . In the late seventies, when the era of dollar omnipotence was only a decade behind, it seemed like a collapse of the verities.'[9] From a European perspective this was bound to cause major economic problems. Both Giscard and Schmidt were critical of American policy, and felt that there had been an abdication of responsibility. Jenkins' role in 1978 – a classic function for the Commission – was to gain agreement that this perception should be the basis for a European initiative to fill the gap. There is a clear contrast with the earlier Werner plan. The first effort at economic and monetary union was torpedoed by external financial pressures. EMS owed its inception to a determination that Europe would evolve a framework for protecting itself against similar pressures in the future.

The new structure was slowly and painfully elaborated in the course of 1978. The centrepiece was a new, although notional, currency – the ECU. Its value would be equivalent to a weighted basket of national currencies. From time to time the weightings would be adjusted according to a complex formula. Henceforth the ECU would be the currency for all internal Community transactions, including the budget. For Community purposes the key exchange rates would be those operating between national currencies and the ECU. Once again there was an attempt to limit exchange rate fluctuations through joint activities by the central banks. However, it was recognised that market pressures could on occasion force a re-alignment. Currencies could be revalued in either direction, but decisions to this effect would be collective rather than national. On the purely monetary side the scheme was a good deal less ambitious than the Werner plan, but it was none the less extending the scope of integration. Recognition was given to the imperative of economic convergence as a prop to exchange rate stability, and some rather meagre resources were allocated to help the weaker economies. Whilst EMS membership was compulsory Britain opted not to join the exchange rate mechanism, an example followed by Greece which joined the Community in 1981.[10]

Final judgement on the success or otherwise of the EMS is complex. It was one of the bases for the commitment in the Maastricht Treaty to Economic and Monetary Union and ultimately a single European currency: prospects for achieving these goals are assessed later.[11] Like the earlier snake in the tunnel, EMS sought to promote monetary integration through currency stability. In neither case was there adequate provision for economic convergence. One indicator of convergence is change in the internal value of national currencies – in other words, the relative rates of inflation. There is a reverse correlation: as economic convergence occurs, differences between national rates of inflation will lessen. Equally the wider those differences, the more compelling the need for effective measures of convergence. In the absence of those measures, significant disparities in inflation levels must inevitably lead to pressures on exchange rates. The problem was recognized and to some extent addressed by agreement that the rules of the EMS would permit agreed changes in exchange rates. However, the degree of actual currency stability would be an obvious litmus paper test of the success of the EMS in progressing monetary integration. There is an interesting table in the book by Dennis Swann which demonstrates the achievements of EMS in managing change and its severe limitations as a mechanism for promoting monetary integration. The table gives the inflation rate and number of currency alignments for each member of the exchange rate mechanism during the 1980s.[12] Italy was the most inflationary and Netherlands the least in a ratio of 4:1. Every currency's value in terms of the ECU was changed at least three times and in some cases as many as six or seven times. In all there were twelve lots of currency revaluations up to January 1990.

However, this alone is not a totally satisfactory way in which to judge EMS. Within its own terms the Jenkins initiative was concerned with seeking a pragmatic solution to the demise of the dollar as world banking currency, the implications for world money markets and the impact on Europe's economy. There was no simple way of returning to the relative certainties of the currency arrangements established in the immediate post-war period. In context, EMS was successful in establishing a framework within which European countries could seek to handle international money flows and could operate the Community in spite of continuing economic divergence. In turbulent times it succeeded in promoting a modicum of monetary stability. EMU was the object of the Werner plan. It is also an objective of the Maastricht treaty. It was at no stage a formal objective of the EMS as established in 1978.

7   From Community to Union

The 1970s witnessed the European Community attempting to synthesise contrasting legacies from its then short history. The achievements – enlargement, EPC and EMS – blended the methodologies of supranationalism and inter-governmentalism. Perhaps this description is a bit too subtle: at the time there was still a strangely prevalent feeling that the Community had somehow lost its way. Efforts to retrieve this position through some kind of relaunch of the integration process helped to turn the Community in on itself.

There were three specific concerns on the agenda in the early 1980s – further enlargement, the ongoing budget problem, institutional reform – and all were largely internal. Yet this was to be the decade which ushered in a major change in the external context, which has always so conditioned the Community. The disintegration and collapse of the Soviet Empire caught Western leaders by surprise. It is worth recalling the centrality of the German problem to the emergence of the communities in the 1950s. When German reunification returned to the political agenda at the end of 1989, Europe's leaders could only react. Nearly forty years after its inception, the very geography of the European Community continued to be conditioned, even determined, by the external international environment. Throughout that period there had been a rhetoric which suggested that Europe could aspire to being a major force in determining that environment. Whilst the Community had clearly become a major international economic player, the political realities continued to differ from that rhetoric! The harsh truth is that the major states of Western Europe were no more pro-active in bringing about the dissolution of the Iron Curtain which split their continent than they had been in its creation. However, this is to jump forward in the analysis: when the new decade began, the major features of the external environment still seemed unchanging and even permanent.

The three concerns itemised above – the continuing row over Britain's contribution to the budget, enlargement and institutional reform – were inevitably linked. Early attempts to find a formula for resolving the budget issue were dogged by failure to recognise the need for a permanent solution rather than a temporary 'fix'.[1] The latter approach ensured that an increasingly irritable Margaret Thatcher was institutionally locked in to raising the issue at successive summits. Consequent explosions of ill temper did nothing to help the Community in its search for solutions to other problems, which included applications for membership from Portugal and Spain.

At the end of the 1970s there were applications for membership on the table from three Mediterranean countries – Greece, Portugal and Spain. Although the subject matter of the negotiations was largely economic, particularly disparities between the three applicants and existing members, the major determinants of the new enlargements were political. Greece had been the earliest European associate of the Community, but the development of a closer relationship was put on hold after a military *coup* overthrew the elected government. The re-establishment of a democratic regime gave the new Greek government critical bargaining power in its bid to join, despite all the economic problems. Whatever their reservations on the readiness of the Greek economy for full membership, member states could hardly fail to offer support to the political aspirations of the new government. The second enlargement – to ten members – took place in January 1981.

Negotiations were rather more protracted with Portugal and Spain. Again there were major economic problems and some member states, particularly France, expressed reservations. However, both countries had been ruled by arbitrary, neo-fascist regimes until the mid 1970s. In the last analysis the establishment of democratic regimes gave their new governments exactly the same political key to membership as Greece, but the economic issues still required resolution.

The third major internal issue confronting the Community was institutional reform. This was a perennial, but the more pressing in view of continued enlargements. The crux of the problem related to voting in the Council of Ministers. Whatever view may be taken of the impact of de Gaulle and the so-called Luxembourg compromise, it is possible to argue that in a Community of only six members, voting methods were not that important. In effect, arguments about the right to national veto could be subsumed within the dynamics of a small, cosy club. This is hardly a view which could be taken of a putative

Community of twelve. Further enlargement necessitated a behavioural change – most likely to be resisted by the United Kingdom, especially if there were no solution to the budgetary problem. At the very beginning of the decade the need for institutional reform generated an interesting, if odd, initiative from Germany and Italy – the so-called Genscher-Colombo plan, named after their respective foreign ministers.[2]

This emerged during 1981, when France was preoccupied with elections which produced a Socialist government with Mitterrand as President. The key features of the plan were development of political co-operation, which would be given an organic link with the Community through the European Council, and a procedure whereby qualified majority voting would be implemented in accordance with the treaty. The plan forms part of the background to the Single European Act, which is discussed below, but initially the auguries for any real change in voting methods did not seem very bright. The Genscher-Colombo plan disappeared into the Solemn Declaration on European Union produced by the Stuttgart European Council in 1983. The latter's vision on majority voting was contained in a somewhat innocuous assertion that 'the application of the decision-making procedures laid down by the Treaties is of vital importance'.[3] However, there were some indications that a solution might in fact be on the way. Early in 1982, under the Belgian Presidency, the annual fixing of farm prices was determined by majority vote against British opposition. An attempt to argue that the decision was contrary to the spirit of the Luxembourg compromise was swept aside, but in truth the British protest was somewhat half-hearted. The incident is a classic of the realities of group decision taking. At the time the UK was seeking Community support over the Argentine invasion of the Falklands, which it quite clearly regarded as being of greater importance than the level of farm prices. Rules of the game determined the outcome rather than the so-called Luxembourg compromise!

This may be to read too much into what was after all a vote on a technical issue. Community dynamics had so far prevented any real challenge to the theory that national interest could be invoked as a basis for veto. Successive British governments considered it a bulwark against supra-nationalism, whilst no French government had yet repudiated the Gaullist legacy. However, Mitterrand's election as President in 1981, followed by a sweeping Socialist triumph in the legislative elections, transformed the French political scene. At first Europe did not appear to be a major governmental priority, but this was to change as domestic economic problems mounted.

It is not easy to weave together the various inititiatives of the early 1980s. A major achievement of the previous decade was agreement to hold direct elections to the European Parliament. These first took place in 1979. Once elected, Parliament not unnaturally sought a rather greater role in the decision-making process with the aspiration of becoming a major Community player. Parliament's decision to focus on the concept of European Union was at least in part a reaction to the Genscher-Colombo plan. Spinelli[4] was the driving force in deliberations which ultimately produced the text of a draft treaty on European Union, handed over to member governments in spring 1984. Much more detailed than Genscher-Colombo or the Solemn Declaration, this was another initiative helping to promote a positive atmosphere for the forthcoming European Council to be held at Fontainebleau in June 1984. France had taken over the the Presidency of the Council in January 1984. Mitterrand clearly already intended to use this position to revive the dynamic of integration, but his approach may well have been influenced by the draft treaty.[5] In May Mitterrand addressed Parliament in his capacity as President of the European Council. A wide-ranging speech included the symbolic commitment that France – progenitor of the Luxembourg compromise – was now willing to embrace majority voting where required.

Earlier, the Genscher-Colombo initiative was characterised as 'odd'. On the German side, it came at a time when the Socialist-led coalition government was running out of steam. France – uninvolved in the initiative , but essential to its success – was preoccupied with domestic issues. By 1984 French priorities had clearly moved, but Mitterrand needed a partner in the new German Chancellor Kohl. Once again the Franco-German alignment would be central to the operation and progress of the Community. In the 1970s there had been a close working partnership between the Socialist Schmidt and the Conservative Giscard. In the 1980s the party politics were reversed as the Christian Democrat Kohl and the Socialist Mitterrand forged an even stronger working relationship. Nothing can better exemplify the centrality of the Franco-German 'axis' in the external politics of the two countries: its impact on the Community was, as ever, decisive.

The European Council at Fontainebleau in June 1984 at last produced a long-term solution to the British budgetary problem. The issue was settled in classic Community style. Budgetary resources were becoming increasingly inadequate and needed to be increased.[6] British agreement was balanced against semi-permanent arrangements for a rebate using a technical formula devised by the Commission. Inter-state bargaining had led to one of the least Community-minded members accepting an extension of integration (higher overall budget) as the means of resolving a problem. Indeed, taken together with the incident over farm prices already discussed, it demonstrates the extent to which even Britain – the apparently ever-reluctant European – had under Margaret Thatcher become sucked into the Community 'game'.

Fontainebleau has to take its place as one of the most significant meetings of the European Council. It resolved a long-standing dispute which was jeopardising progress on a whole range of issues, cleared the way for Spanish and Portugese accession, and set in motion the process which was to lead to the signature of the Single European Act (SEA). None of this could have happened without agreement between France and Germany. Fontainebleau marked the re-emergence of what was earlier termed the 'Franco-German axis'. Removal of the long-standing budgetary problem obviated the danger that Britain would simply obstruct all progress, and this brought one immediate bonus. Even though Thatcher's predilections and policy priorities ensured that Britain would still not normally be centre stage, she was heavily committed to the notion of 'completing' the Community as a trading and commercial entity by establishing a single market. In the short run, Thatcher could thus work with Mitterrand and Kohl on what may be considered the first phase in their mission to regenerate the Community. They also gained a major long-term ally in the person of Jacques Delors, whose appointment as the next Commission President was also agreed at Fontainebleau.

The term 'founding fathers' is normally used in a Community context to refer to those who inspired the original treaties in the fifties and who led the institutions at the commencement of the process of integration. As the Community developed thereafter, many individuals played important roles, but it is hard to think of occasions prior to the appointment of Delors where any were indispensable, save perhaps for Roy Jenkins in the case of the establishment of EMS. Delors, a former civil servant and government minister, was to be President of the Commission for a decade, which witnessed the SEA and the implementation of the 1992 programme, the Maastricht Treaty on European Union, the inclusion of Portugal and Spain and successful negotiations for membership of Austria, Finland and Sweden. A convinced federalist, Delors was to become virtually synonymous with the Community during the decade 1985–95.

With the three largest countries onside, it was logical for the new Commission to make the single market its major policy priority when it took office at the beginning of 1985. The establishment of internal free trade, theoretically achieved back in the 1960s, meant the abolition of all barriers. In practice, the latter had remained a pious aspiration so long as a whole host of technical, fiscal and other barriers existed. Early in 1985 the Commission produced a white paper on establishing a single market. This, together with the report by the Dooge Committee, established at Fontainebleau to examine institutional issues, formed the major agenda when the European Council met in Milan in late June 1985 and took the crucial decisions which were to lead to the negotiation and signature of SEA.

The Milan European Council was an early demonstration of the new Franco-German axis. Analysis of these events should properly focus on three critical features. First, the European Council confirmed its assumption of direct responsibility for all major decisions. In 1984 this involved enlargement and the budget. In 1985 it embraced 'completion' of the Community itself in the shape of the single market. Second, the actual decision to hold an inter-governmental conference (IGC), which would give a treaty base to foreign policy co-operation and revise some of the institutional arrangements, was taken by a majority despite opposition from Britain, Denmark and Greece. Italian Prime Minister Craxi as President of the European Council played a key role in this. Third, despite objections to developing European structures and institutions, Britain attached sufficient importance to the single market to accept a majority decision on the IGC.

The lead up to the IGC had been long and tortuous, but the actual negotiation of the SEA was relatively simple. The IGC met in September, and by January an agreed text had emerged. The treaty itself is analysed in the next chapter. Its main features were agreement to implement the single market by the end of 1992, the establishment of a legal basis for Political Co-operation and a number of institutional reforms. Whilst not formally repudiating the Luxembourg compromise with its apparent extension of the national veto, member states seemed to have reached some understanding that in future the spirit of the original treaties would apply. The point is underlined by the fact that virtually all the provisions relating to the single market would be implemented by majority vote.

In the immediate aftermath of the ratification of the SEA, some observers drew attention to the gap between aspirations expressed by Parliament in its Draft Treaty and the actual achievement.[7] Although true, such comments are wide of the mark. In the negotiating process Parliament was little more than a bystander with the right to be heard. The member states were anxious to achieve a relaunching of the move towards unification after a period of apparent stagnation, and they used the carrot of the advantages of a single market to try to convince the sceptics. As the next chapter will show, the SEA foreshadowed virtually the entire contents of the later Maastricht Treaty on European Union, but ratification of the latter was much more difficult once the detail was spelled out. Any notion that Maastricht could somehow have been brought forward by five years is quite unreal. Whilst ratification by all members, including Portugal and Spain who joined the Community on 1 January 1986, was never in any real doubt, the Danish Parliament or Folketing actually rejected the Treaty – a decision overturned by a subsequent referendum.

With the ratification of the SEA, Community developments become part of contemporary history. As our own perspectives shift, analysis of cause and effect becomes that much more difficult. In the period between the SEA and the Treaty on European Union, the major internal factor affecting the Community was the commitment to implement the single market. The way in which the idea of the single market captured public imagination is unrivalled by any other Community initiative since its beginning in the fifties. Some excitement was even generated by the notion of implementation by a particular year. Back in Chapter 2 reference was made to functionalism, and also to some of the early academics who wrote about the integration process. According to Ernst Haas,[8] the functional approach to integration was all about the transfer of loyalties and expectations from the nation states to the new supra-national institutions. Some thirty years later, the single market initiative is almost a classic of functionalist strategy. In the immediate aftermath of the signature and ratification of the SEA, the major task was to bring about implementation of the single market by the end of 1992. The single market programme involved a vast amount of technical work leading to a plethora of legislative measures. This in turn brought the Commission back to centre stage perhaps for the first time since the crises of the mid 1960s.

At the time of the Milan European Council, the Commission had presented a white paper on the implementation of a single market. With the signature of the new treaty, it fell to the Commission to draft some 300 legislative measures and to seek to steer them through the Council. This process was to mark the emergence of Delors as a major 'player' in the Community and as perhaps the most significant President of the Commission: certainly the first to become almost a 'household name'.

A major obstacle to implementation of the single market was posed by the economic gap between richer and poorer states. The southern or Mediterranean members argued that the commitment to cohesion enshrined in the SEA had to be implemented as a precondition for the single market programme. The Commission responded by proposing a package of measures. These would necessitate a significant increase in the budget, a prospect which met with little enthusiasm on the part of richer northern members who would have to pay the bill. The issue was resolved during Germany's Presidency of the Council in the first part of 1988. In effect, Germany agreed to meet the bulk of the bill in order to secure implementation of the single market. It was a critical moment in Chancellor Kohl's elevation to the rank of European statesman. It also consolidated his alignment with a re-elected President Mitterrand and ultimately opened up the route which would lead to Maastricht.[9]

The central thesis of this book is that external events have always been a critical determinant of the process of integration. However, the declared perspectives of the principal players at the time may not be the best guide to this. So far this chapter has focused entirely on internal Community events, completely ignoring the external context. At one level it seems almost unfair to make the point that whilst the Community was largely absorbed with the single market and with the pre-negotiations which were to lead to the Maastricht Treaty, the external context was entirely and irrevocably changed by collapse of the Communist regimes in Central and Eastern Europe, the dismantling of the USSR and the end of the Iron Curtain and the Cold War. The consequential reunification of Germany meant a physical and geographical enlargement of the Community itself.

The collapse of the Communist regimes and the disintegration of the Soviet Empire were unexpected events. It is easy enough to understand in retrospect why these developments took place, and some will argue that they were inevitable, but at the time of the SEA there was no statesman in Western Europe with any conception that the external context was about to change so rapidly. It is interesting to contrast the prevalent external context at the time of the signature of the Treaty of Paris establishing the European Coal and Steel Community with that pertaining at the time of Maastricht. In the first case the external context, whilst immensely threatening, was known and established. The Treaty of Paris was a considered response to an ongoing situation. In the second case, the international climate was less threatening, but also far newer and less stable. The year 1989 was one of revolutionary changes throughout Central and Eastern Europe; Germany was reunited in 1990; the attempted *coup* which finally destroyed both the USSR and Soviet-style Communism took place in August 1990. Ultimately, these events will have a profound effect on the future development and overall direction of what is now the European Union,[10] but their immediate impact has to be looked at in a different light. There was no shortage of speeches, and presumably internal memoranda, drawing attention to the significance of events beyond the Eastern border, but it is hard to see what practical difference they actually made in the short term to policies being pursued by the member states or to the development of the Community. The process which would lead to the Maastricht Treaty on European Union was set in motion in the first part of 1988. The treaty itself was signed at the end of 1991. There is no evidence that this process would have proceeded differently even if none of the events to the East had occurred!

In concluding this chapter it may be appropriate to summarise the major events which led up to the Maastricht Treaty and its subsequent ratification. Although implementation of the single market brought the Commission to the centre stage, the real driving force for developing the Community was undoubtedly the European Council. In the course of 1988 and 1989 it agreed to establish two separate but parallel IGCs to consider respectively Political Union and Economic and Monetary Union. After some preparations, the two IGCs came into formal existence at the Rome European Council in December 1990. Working throughout 1991 they reported to the Maastricht European Council just one year later, resulting in the Treaty on European Union.

Inevitably the attitudes of France and Germany were crucial. Initially there was some difference of emphasis. Once German reunification was secured, Kohl's major aim was to complete the process of locking the newly united Germany irrevocably into an integrated Europe through Political Union. Mitterrand's concern was the pre-eminence of the Deutschmark and the desirability of establishing some European political control over monetary issues. By mid 1990 the positions of the two chief partners were broadly in line, henceforth working towards both political and economic and monetary union, with strong support from Italy, who took over the Council Presidency in the second half of the year.

Meanwhile ,British policy was in turmoil. Following her third successive election victory, Thatcher became increasingly strident in her condemnation of further European integration. This was undoubtedly fuelled by growing concern over possible German dominance. However, many of Thatcher's leading ministers were committed to extending the European agenda. During 1989 the British government both agreed that at last it would join the exchange rate mechanism and vainly opposed the establishment of the IGC on EMU. Late in 1990, following the resignation of Geoffrey Howe as Foreign Minister, essentially on issues concerned with Europe, Thatcher was deposed as Prime Minister. At first sight it is an interesting example of a reverse linkage between national and European developments. This book has highlighted a number of occasions when the course of European integration was profoundly influenced, even determined, by national political developments. The deposition of Thatcher was an occasion on which European issues apparently impacted decisively on national politics. However, occasion and cause are not always synonymous and the reality is slightly different. European issues were undoubtedly the occasion for the change of Prime Minister. However, the underlying causes lay in domestic politics – particularly the poll tax fiasco – and a fear amongst Conservative back-benchers that the next general election could be lost if changes were not made. There is little evidence that the replacement of Margaret Thatcher by John Major changed British attitudes towards the Community, soon to become the Union. Differences between leading British government ministers remained and splits over European issues in the Conservative party were to deepen, especially after the 1992 elections. Other European leaders now had to deal with a much weaker British Prime Minister – not necessarily an advantage.

Although there is little evidence that the changed external context had much impact on the IGCs and the shape of the Treaty on European Union, the same may not necessarily be true for developments immediately post-Maastricht. The ratification process was more difficult than that for any other treaty. A referendum in Denmark rejected the entire Treaty, a situation only reversed by special concessions and opt outs. President Mitterand called a referendum in France, largely in the hope of boosting his own waning popularity, and came within a whisker of losing. In Britain the ratification process in Parliament was delayed by the growing split in the Conservative party re-inforced by a crisis in the European Monetary System. When Britain had finally joined the exchange rate mechanism in 1990, the pound sterling – which had for some time previously been shadowing the mark – was valued at a high rate which simply could not be sustained. Faced with enormous and uncontrollable speculative movements and unwilling to seek an agreed currency revaluation, Britain simply pulled out of the exchange rate mechanism in September 1992. Thereafter with the Conservative party increasingly adopting the line on Europe which had theoretically cost Thatcher her job, ratification of Maastricht was for some time on a knife edge.

This chapter is entitled 'From Commmunity to Union'. An apparent relaunching of the integration process with the single market initiative promoted another of those relatively brief and infrequent waves of what has in earlier chapters been termed 'Europhoria'. The relaunched integration process seemingly culminated in successful negotiation of the Treaty on European Union. Nonetheless this chapter ends with a question mark. The problems of ratifying the new treaty suggest the recurrence of a basic doubt about where Europe should be going. Earlier it was argued that there was little clear linkage between external context and the process leading to Maastricht. However, the external context is never far away. By the time the new treaty was signed in February 1992, the revolutionary events in Central and Eastern Europe and the USSR were not quite so new. Perceptions of a new and very different international order were beginning to make an impact on the thinking of both opinion formers and the general public. Real questions could be asked about the contemporary relevance of a structure originally designed to meet the problems of the 1950s. There is no necessary suggestion that all the critics of the new Treaty were motivated by this argument, but it needs to be assessed. This will be the task of the final chapter of this book. However, before then there is a need to consider in more detail the treaty which transformed the Community into the Union.

8 Maastricht and European Union

Throughout the changing contexts of European integration it has been commonplace for both academic observers and active practitioners to argue that Community institutions are in urgent need of overhaul.[1] Chapter 4 looked at the original institutional structure of the Community, carrying it forward to 1986 to take account of the first three series of enlargements. It was possible to do this because that institutional structure remained – at least in a formal sense – largely unchanged until the Single European Act (SEA) of 1986 and the 1992 Treaty on European Union. In the twenty years which elapsed between the treaty which merged the institutions of the three communities and the SEA, the only significant formal structural change resulted from the 'own resources' treaties which gave Parliament significant additional powers and as a result tilted the balance slightly between the major institutions. By way of contrast, direct elections of the Parliament did not immediately change the power balance. During this time, however, a number of extra-treaty institutions or arrangements emerged – Council Presidency, Council Secretariat, European Political Co-operation, European Council. These developed iteratively, but they all had a considerable impact on how the Community worked in practice. They were only brought under the formal legal structural umbrella by the SEA and the Treaty on European Union.

The present chapter is in a sense the mirror opposite of Chapter 4. In the earlier chapter the process of integration was placed in the context of the preoccupations of the 1950s. However, a forward-looking view was taken of the evolution of the institutions up to the mid 1980s. The main focus of the present chapter is the two new treaties and extension of the scope of integration reflected in the creation of the European Union. Since so much of the context for the recent changes arises from consideration of institutional performance, the chapter will begin by looking backwards and attempting an analytical over-view of the development of the institutions from the Treaty of Paris to the SEA.

There are a number of contrasting approaches to this analysis. An initial view is that the European entity is built solely on law or treaty. 'Europe', unlike its state components, is not part of the natural, rational world which we have inherited. It lacks the inherent legitimacy and sovereignty which we assume to be endemic to nation states. The EC came into existence with the specific act of signing treaties at particular times. Those treaties adumbrated principles and established mechanisms for decision making. A broad structure is laid down with clear roles for each of the major institutions. Everything which happens in the communities has to have a legal, treaty-based foundation.

Until the mid 1960s few questioned this legalistic approach, but thereafter another view began gradually to be superimposed. Precisely because the Community had many of the characteristics of a club with a restricted membership, it began to devise ways of working outside the narrow limits of codified rules. Hence the notion of 'rules of the game' as an explanation of how the Community actually operated.[2] Confronted with problems, members not infrequently found themselves in an institutional impasse. Provided that there was some political will for a solution, the same members began to show increasing flexibility in seeking alternative approaches. This is a partial explanation of the emergence of those extra-treaty institutions mentioned above. What is particularly interesting is that the notion of 'rules of the game' began to emerge through the major crisis of the 1960s. They are in many ways a much better explanation of how decisions were actually reached in the Council than any reference to the arrangements which ended that crisis.[3]

It is almost tautologous to argue that 'rules of the game' can only work if participants are committed to playing the game itself. Until the first enlargement, this was the case: there was a real sense in which the Six formed a small and cosy club. However, this began to break down once newcomers joined who had never shared the original objectives of the Six. The founders of the treaty assumed that shared political will would be a route through problems – European unification would always transcend other national interests. Even for Gaullist France in the mid 1960s this remained largely true. However, once Britain joined, the notion of a cosy club began to fall apart. It is doubtful if any British government has fully accepted the 'Community method' as a means of transacting business. In some cases they may not even have understood the concept. Certainly none since that of Edward Heath has even given lip-service to the belief – which is still widely held in many member states – that unification is the most important of a series of competing national interests. A new element thus crept into Community bargaining, with a corresponding increase in institutional stress. An alternative way of looking at the new extra-treaty creations is that they could be posited as replacement for, rather than reinforcement of, the communities themselves.

The major focus of this chapter is the Maastricht Treaty, which covers the entire scope of relations between member states and aspires to convert them, including the Community, into a European Union. Maastricht is much the most ambitious European treaty since the 1950s. However, before examining it in detail, there is a need to consider its immediate predecessor, the 1986 Single European Act (SEA). As mentioned in the previous chapter, the SEA was received with considerable enthusiasm at the time, mainly because of the commitment to implementing the single market by the end of 1992. Relatively successful accomplishment of this task may be one reason why the SEA was almost forgotten once the Treaty on European Union was signed. Yet, as was pointed out in the previous chapter, the former, much shorter treaty foreshadowed a great deal that was to be included in Maastricht.

The centrepiece of the SEA was the proposal to establish a unified single internal market to ensure completely free movement of goods, persons, services and capital by the end of 1992. This commitment to the single market was the major determinant of the SEA and certainly it offered the chief public relations focus. However, the SEA was also a first tangible expression of more than ten years' discussion of some kind of relaunch for the European institutions. It specifically takes as starting point the 1983 Stuttgart declaration, with its commitment to European Union. Unlike Maastricht, the SEA is a short treaty. In it the twelve seek to tidy and codify the scope of integration. Significantly, however, it also extends beyond the legal confines of the communities to consider other aspects of relations between member states.

The core commitment is to an internal market comprising 'an area without internal frontiers in which the free movement of goods, persons, services and capital is ensured'. The Commission would make proposals for the implementation of this commitment and the Council would decide by qualified majority, save for issues concerned with harmonisation of legislation on indirect taxation, which would require unanimity. The commitment to use majority voting on these issues is symbolic of the new approach enshrined in the SEA. As mentioned in the previous chapter, there was at the same time an unwritten under-standing between member states that majority voting would be more widely used – in effect, treaty provisions would be implemented and the Luxembourg compromise would no longer be cited.

The SEA also extends the competence of the Community in a number of other ways. Perhaps the most important are measures to ensure economic and social cohesion. Although the treaty does not use the word 'convergence' in this context, it does speak of promoting 'overall harmonious development', 'reducing disparities' and redressing 'the principal regional imbalances'. All these are directly linked to the implementation of the single market.

The second major feature of the SEA lies in the provision for the first time of a treaty basis for European Political Co-operation (EPC). Even if the essence of EPC remains consultation, it rests henceforth on legal commitment and ceases to be voluntary. Ministers of Foreign Affairs are required to meet four times a year for EPC purposes, and they are formally permitted to discuss such business even when meeting as the Council of the EC. The Commission and Parliament both have the right to be involved in political co-operation. The object of EPC is the formulation and implementation of a common foreign policy. Members also express an aspiration for closer co-operation on issues of European security. The locking together of Community and EPC is reinforced by another institutional development. For the first time a treaty text gives formal recognition to the existence of the European Council, which is required to meet at least twice a year. Interestingly, the treaty is silent about the functions of the European Council – this had to wait on Maastricht.

The SEA also extends the competence of the Community in a number of other ways. The most important concern co-operation to ensure convergence of economic and monetary policies; harmonisa-tion of measures to achieve health and safety at work; research and technical development and environmental protection. None of these is spelled out in any great detail.

Finally, the SEA also seeks to tackle the so-called 'democratic deficit'. A central feature of the ethos of the Community is commit-ment to democratic government. However, the major power brokers – Commission and Council of Ministers – are not directly elected, whilst the original treaties severely circumscribed the role of the European Parliament. In one sense the introduction of direct elections under-scored the imbalance. As a result of the SEA, Parliament became for the first time a key player in the legislative process through the intro-duction of a 'co-operation procedure', not dissimilar to that used for part of the budget. Parliament was given the right to propose legislative amendments, although the final word still rests with the Council. The new procedure applied to measures to outlaw discrimination on grounds of nationality; free movement of workers; right of establishment; harmonisation of laws; aspects of social co-operation; and certain issues concerned with the European Investment Bank.

One of the final clauses of the SEA commits members to a review of political co-operation after five years. This is one obvious link to Maastricht. The Treaty on European Union is clearly much more ambitious, but it does not go that far into areas not already foreshadowed by the SEA. Indeed, it is not an exaggeration to suggest that the later treaty contains very little that is conceptually new.

The idea of transforming relations between member states into a Union dates from October 1972.[4] Despite a plethora of declarations, investigations, committees and reports, there was no substantial progress until the SEA 'resolved to implement this European Union on the basis, firstly, of the Communities ... and, secondly, of European Co-operation'. At one stage it seemed feasible to consider a new Treaty of Rome, which would again give the European edifice a clear legal framework for all activities. Any such notion evaporated in the absence of consensus as to the goals and purpose of such a Union, and the extremely uneven progress made in developments in different facets of its (the Union's) contents. The piecemeal, iterative approach to unification and the development of extra non-treaty-based institutions clearly promote a need for overall codification, but there can no longer be any assumption of automatic political will for the process of unification. The inter-governmental committees which preceded Maastricht were simply unable to produce an agreement on a comprehensive, over-arching framework for European Union.

At Maastricht the member states 'decided to establish a European Union'. The Union has four objectives: promotion of economic and social progress, facilitated by economic and monetary union; implementation of a common foreign and security policy; co-operation in justice and home affairs; and establishment of joint citizenship. The problem is that the pace of integration would vary in these different areas. Most members were anxious to avoid diluting existing Community arrangements. This is demonstrated by article C, which gives a ringing and somewhat misleading declaration: 'The Union shall be served by a single institutional framework which shall ensure the consistency and continuity of the activities carried out in order to attain the objectives while respecting and building upon the "acquis communautaire".' In practice, the dilemma is resolved through the concept of a series of so-called 'pillars' with their own institutional arrangements. Co-ordination of the Union is the responsibility of the European Council, which is at last given a treaty-based role to 'provide the Union with the necessary impetus for its development'. One possible interpretation is that the European Council is the only specific Union institution. The three pillars are the European Community;[5] common foreign and security policy; and arrangements regarding justice and home affairs. In effect, there are three different areas of joint activity, each with its own procedures. As will be shown, the two non-Community pillars are based largely on inter-governmental co-operation.

On this analysis, European Union is little more than the umbrella term for a disparate collection of agreements and commitments. The actual treaty establishing the Union is an extremely complex document, much of which is concerned with amending the EEC Treaty, which in turn becomes almost incomprehensible. The most important of these changes and additions fall into four categories: institutional amendments; citizenship; economic and monetary union; and social policy.

The major institutional changes involve inclusion of the doctrine of subsidiarity and a significant increase in the legislative powers of the European Parliament. Subsidiarity is effectively defined by a new treaty article:

> In areas which do not fall within its exclusive competence, the Community shall take action, in accordance with the principle of subsidiarity, only if and in so far as the objectives of the proposed action cannot be sufficiently achieved by the Member States and can therefore .... be better achieved by the Community.

Various claims have been made as to the origin and ownership of this principle. Historically it looms larger in theological than in political literature, which has not averted a claim that 'subsidiarity is a traditional federalist concept'.[6] On the other hand, it was the anti-federalist British government which insisted on its inclusion in the treaty.

It is difficult to see how this doctrine (new for the Community) is likely to have much impact in practice. The British government claimed that acceptance of the principle of subsidiarity was a major historic reversal of the onward march of integration. The implication is that national action and national policies would now be the norm: only where these were inadequate to resolve problems would the Community become involved. It is hard to see how this could affect the legal powers of the European institutions as defined in the treaties. In any event, disputes could only be resolved by the Court of Justice, which is itself an institution operating at European level. In practice, such a dispute would only arise if a majority of countries insisted on taking action at European level and had the voting power to carry the day. The aggrieved minority could then presumably appeal to the Court. However, under such circumstances the Court would be hardly likely to wish be involved in what would be a purely political question. The position might seem to be different where it was proposed to grant new powers to the Community institutions. Henceforth any member state expressing reluctance could refer to subsidiarity as a justification for opposition. However, in a political sense this changed nothing. New powers always require treaty amendments which necessitate unanimity or, at least consensus – with or without the doctrine of subsidiarity. It is difficult to resist the conclusion that subsidiarity would become just another point of reference to aid the rhetoric of debate at times of controversy – along with the 'acquis communautaire' and the 'Luxembourg compromise' which have been discussed in earlier chapters.

The other major institutional change involved extensions to the power of the European Parliament. Perhaps the most important is that parliamentary approval is now required for appointment of the Commission. This gives a kind of quasi-governmental status to the Commission and it brings Parliament closer to the national pattern. Changes to the legislative process are much more complex. The co-operation procedure introduced by the SEA allowed Parliament to propose specific amendments to legislation being considered by the Council. Maastricht makes a further change to the legislative process. On certain issues – notably free movement of people, the internal market, consumer protection – Parliament now has co-equal powers with the Council: the agreement of both is required for legislation.[7] Some of these had been subject to the co-operation procedure under the SEA. However, Maastricht also retains and extends both the co-operation procedure and the original consultation mechanism for different areas of legislation. It also lays down that parliamentary assent is needed for international agreements and on matters relating to European citizenship.

It is worth commenting on the role Parliament now has in the decision-making process. Depending on the issue to hand, Parliament is either simply informed *or* it is formally consulted *or* it may suggest amendments without having the final word *or* it shares equally in the process and its agreement is required *or* its assent is necessary and it has a veto.[8] This is so grotesquely complicated as to be incomprehensible: it can only undermine any notion of Community democracy. It is a normal requirement for an effective and functioning democracy that voters have some understanding of the powers of those they elect and the process by which decisions are taken. Under Maastricht this is virtually impossible.

The concept of European citizenship is a major innovation of Maastricht, although it is actually introduced by an amendment to the EEC Treaty. Nationals of member countries are citizens of the Union, with rights and duties resulting from the various treaties. It is worth noting that 'rights' and 'duties' are novel concepts in terms of the unwritten British constitution. European citizens are free to move and live anywhere within the Union boundaries. They are also entitled to diplomatic protection outside Europe by the authorities of any member country. Citizens of the European Union will be entitled to vote in local and European elections in the country of their residence, regardless of nationality. In the event of complaints against Community institutions they will also have recourse to a European ombudsman appointed by Parliament.

The largest section of amendments/additions is concerned with economic and monetary policy, the scope of which now goes far beyond anything envisaged in the original EEC Treaty, although the commitments all flow logically from the European Monetary System and the SEA. Members are required to co-ordinate their economic policies. This includes limiting budgetary deficits – enforceable by Council sanctions. Price and exchange rate stability are equally matters of common concern. Where member states encounter balance-of-payments difficulties, the Commission will recommend the action to be taken. The intention is to bring about economic harmonisation or convergence during an interim period prior to the establishment of full economic and monetary union by the beginning of 1999 at the latest. A European Clearing Bank will then become responsible for establishing a single European currency.

In terms of both national sovereignty and psychology, the Maastricht clauses on Economic and Monetary Union may well represent the biggest single leap forward for European integration since the signature of the Treaty of Paris. Full implementation transfers authority over virtually all aspects of economic and monetary policy to the EC. This is the background to the protocol which gives the UK the right to opt out of the final stage, including the common currency. However, a further protocol binds all members to facilitate the attainment of Economic and Monetary Union for the Community as a whole. At the Edinburgh summit a year after the Treaty on European Union was signed and after the first adverse Danish referendum, it was agreed that Denmark would not participate in the final stage of economic and monetary union. The implications of these two potential national opt-outs will be considered later.

The final major addition to the EC Treaty concerns social policy. In 1989 the European Council adopted a Social Charter. In essence, this was a declaration of intent, although the Commission sought to reinforce it through an action programme. The British government, ideologically opposed to any increase in state intervention in social issues, declined to participate. In the run-up to Maastricht it became clear that there was an unbridgeable divide between the British government and the other eleven over extending the social activities of the Community. As a result, social policy is handled through a protocol to the treaty, which is sometimes referred to as the 'Social Chapter'. In it the member states agree collectively to allow the eleven (fourteen after the enlargement of 1995 to include Austria, Finland and Sweden) to make use of Community institutions and procedures in order to implement the substantive agreement on social policy. The agreement, annexed to the protocol, incorporates the Social Charter into the treaty and commits those member countries to the promotion of employment; improvement in working conditions, including health and safety; and equal pay. Social security, redundancy conditions and collective bargaining likewise become issues of common concern. As with economic and monetary union the British opt-out raises the possibility of a two-speed or 'à la carte' Europe.

The scale and complexities of this restructuring of the Community dwarf the other two pillars of Maastricht. However, there is a sense in which ultimate judgement of the success of European Union will be conditioned by progress in these two, newer areas. After all, they are key indicators of the extent to which the Union is more than the Community writ large. In the SEA, members did no more than agree 'to formulate and implement a European foreign policy'. Maastricht grandiloquently announces that 'a common foreign and security policy is hereby established'. A number of general objectives are laid down: to safeguard the values and interests of the Union; to strengthen security; to preserve peace; to promote international co-operation; and to develop and consolidate democracy, the rule of law and respect for freedom. Further definition and implementation are for later. Prior to Maastricht, decisions on political co-operation were taken by meetings of foreign ministers – in effect, the same people as attended the Community's Council of Ministers. In this respect Maastricht offers clarification. Effectively, the work of defining common policies in the foreign and security field becomes the responsibility of the Council of Ministers subject to overall co-ordination by the European Council. The treaty also includes a somewhat veiled allusion in a protocol to the prospect of deciding such issues by majority vote: 'Member States will, to the extent possible, avoid preventing a unanimous decision where a qualified majority exists in favour of that decision.' The Commission and the European Parliament are entitled to some involvement but they have no real power and fairly little influence on decision making under this pillar. Finally, members are also committed to the principle of establishing a common defence policy in association with the Western European Union (WEU). It is difficult to be precise about what this will mean in practice, since the policy must respect obligations under NATO as well as the defence orientation of member states which had hitherto been neutral.

The third and final pillar of the Union concerns Justice and Home Affairs. This covers movement across frontiers, asylum, police and judicial co-operation. There is very much less pre-history to this pillar than is the case with foreign policy and security. During the run-up to the SEA, some member countries began to discuss the possibilities and implications of removing controls on the movement of people in parallel with the establishment of the single market. In 1985 Belgium, France, Germany, Luxembourg and the Netherlands signed the Schengen agreement to facilitate this objective through a substantial removal of internal customs and passport controls. Nothing seemed to come of this for a long time. In 1990 there was a further detailed agreement on the implementation of Schengen. Even then, a further five years were to elapse before it came into effect. None the less, Schengen is part of the relevant background to the third pillar. There is a linkage to the concept of citizenship established by amendment to the EEC Treaty (see above). The key right of the European citizen to move freely throughout the Union can only be ensured through the emergence of common rules under the third pillar.

Despite this, the treaty commitment is only to inform and consult. Once again, it is for the appropriate Council of Ministers to promote joint action and further co-operation. The extent to which Justice and Home Affairs are handled by inter-governmental procedures is reinforced by further clauses. There is a co-ordinating committee of national officials to advise the Council which can normally only act through unanimity. The Council may recommend to member states the adoption of new conventions detailing further co-operation. Measures to implement such conventions would require support of two-thirds of the member states – a different voting procedure from that used in the Community. As with the previous pillar, Commission and Parliament are involved but have little influence.

Although the Treaty on European Union had been twenty years in gestation, it was hailed by Europhiles as the beginning of a new era in integration. Difficulties in the ratification process somewhat dented this euphoria. In addition, the British opt-outs on economic and monetary union and the social protocol marked a new departure. Hitherto it had been argued that participation was an 'all or nothing' affair. A prime condition of membership was acceptance of all of the ever-evolving 'acquis communautaire'. At Maastricht, Britain succeeded in eroding that principle, although at a price. Hitherto it had also been accepted that new developments going beyond existing treaty commitments required the agreement of all. The British government in effect traded a 'veto' for an opt-out. Within a year the precedent had been followed to ensure Danish acceptance of Maastricht after the first adverse referendum. These potential opt-outs clearly raise the possibility of a two-speed or 'à la carte' Europe in which the core of the Union/Community accept the 'acquis' but other members only participate in some activities. The final part of this chapter analyses the opt-outs and explores their implications.

The two British opt-outs are specified in the Treaty. Britain is not a party to the social chapter and reserves the right not to participate in the third and final stage of economic and monetary union. Danish opt-outs are based on an inter-governmental agreement reached at the Edinburgh meeting of the European Council in December 1992. This agreement contains a number of explanatory statements made by the Council and by the Danish government. A good deal of this could be considered as window dressing to help the latter in its domestic battles. However, Denmark will not participate in the third stage of economic and monetary union and will not take part in the evolution of defence policy. In connection with the latter, Denmark undertakes not to seek to prevent closer co-operation on defence. This is another example of trading a possible veto for an opt-out.

In considering the impact of these opt-outs, there are two key questions. Do they make evolution of common policies and attainment of the Union's goals more or less likely? And what are the implications for the Union of non-participation by certain member states? The Danish defence opt-out can be dealt with fairly swiftly. There are in practice no real teeth to the Maastricht commitment to seek to find a basis for common policy. The need to embrace the interests of both NATO members and the neutrals suggests that policy evolution will be slow and limited. In the immediate post-Cold War era, the purposes of defence policy also require re-evaluation. This will be one theme of the next chapter. At Maastricht the member states agreed that there would be a further Inter-governmental Conference in 1996 to review progress and consider further developments. In the intermediate period there was no substantive progress on defence issues as far as the European Union itself was concerned.[10]

During those same years issues concerning EMU have been much more immediate. Attainment of the necessary degree of economic convergence raises a range of problems which can only be overcome through a high level of political commitment. It is worth re-emphasising the point that Britain and Denmark have not opted out of the commitment to economic convergence which is necessary for implementation of the final stage of EMU. The opt-outs do apply to the final stage: in Britain's case it is the right to make a decision whether or not to participate, whilst Denmark has already decided. It will be necessary to return to this issue in the final, concluding chapter. Here it is worth making the point that the opt-outs may in a sense marginalise the two most sceptical members who will, therefore, have limited input to policy elaboration. Denmark remains committed to exchange rate collaboration, whilst the British position is obscure. In practice, though, it is hard to see how either country could remain outside a system applying to the rest of the Community without even further marginalisation. Quite apart from the political sensitivities, the biggest objection to EMU and the proposed single currency lies in the difficulty of meeting the convergence criteria. A tentative conclusion is that, whatever the prospects for the Community moving to a single currency at some point, they may be marginally enhanced by the opt-outs. And if they are successful, there is unlikely in practice to be a two-speed Union for very long.

The issue of the social protocol is slightly different. Britain is clearly the odd man out. Indeed, some countries, including Denmark, consider the social provisions to be too mild. The basis for the British opt-out was partly ideological and partly a fear of increased industrial costs. In so far as there is any credibility to the second, it seems unlikely that the other members would allow Britain a competitive advantage through non-compliance with the evolving rules. The other fourteen member states are able to use Community resources and procedures to implement policy and they may well be able to pressurise Britain into ultimately renouncing the opt-out. However, this will not be necessary since the Labour Party which swept back to power at the 1997 British general election in May 1997 has a very different attitude towards social policy and the Maastricht social chapter. Indeed a commitment to sign up to the social chapter was expressed within days of the formation of the Blair government and this will happen within the context of the work of the IGC set up to review Maastricht.

During their long years of opposition the Labour Party's attitude towards Community and Union has undergone a massive change. Immediately after 1979 antipathy towards the whole European project became ever more pronounced, especially after the formation of the Social Democratic Party. Had a Labour government been elected in the mid 1980s it would to all intents and purposes have been committed to withdrawal. Catastrophic electoral defeats, the dynamic of a two party system in which Conservative governments increasingly occupied the so-called Eurosceptic ground, modernization and policy reform within the Labour Party brought about a major change. By the time Tony Blair became Prime Minister, Labour was considerably more favourably disposed towards European integration than the outgoing Conservative administration. For the first time since 1974 a British government seemed genuine in proclaiming an intent to be at the centre of developments in the Community/Union.

Whilst the actual dynamics of the electoral campaign make it unlikely that even the new Labour government would be willing to sign up for implementation by 1999 of EMU, this is not likely to be the key issue for the IGC. During the mid 1990s attainment of the convergence criteria by more than a handful of member states has seemed increasingly unlikely. The economic and political implications of seeking to achieve the criteria have placed strains on many national governments. The policy of the new British government is likely to be based on pragmatic rather than ideological grounds.

In this context the notion of a two speed Europe implies a core group of countries moving to the final stage of EMU with others following behind. There would be a need for structured links between the two groups. The removal of the major ideological challenge to EMU itself is likely to focus attention on such pragmatic issues. It also makes it more likely that some kind of fudge will emerge which will include a re-affirmed commitment to the goal for the entire membership whilst in practice slowing down implementation.

9 Conclusion
Towards a federal Europe

The major thesis of this book is that the establishment and development of the European Community can only be assessed and understood in the context of both the wider international environment and the domestic economics and politics of actual and potential member states. The process of integration was a specific European response to the external context – issues of war and peace, the German problem and the then new bipolar world. Subsequent developments within the Community have been a function of the normal maelstrom of political ideas and concepts, but the key decisions to extend the process of integration have always been based on realism and practical politics. Successive governments of France and the Netherlands – two founder members of the Community – have not differed from successive governments of Britain and Denmark – notorious Eurosceptics – in making so-called 'national interest' a first priority in their involvement in international issues in general and European construction in particular. The difference is that the former, unlike the latter, have normally seen the development of European integration and the processes of supra-nationalism as a quintessential part of that national interest.

In a book which is dealing with contemporary politics and history, a final chapter needs both to offer a synthesis and to look forward. The Maastricht Treaty on European Union committed members to a further inter-governmental conference which would start work in 1996 with a view to revising/progressing the Union. It is tempting to devote much of this final, concluding chapter of this book to consideration of issues likely to dominate the IGC and to use this as a basis for assessing the future direction of the Union. However, keeping faith with the major thesis of this book necessitates a broader approach concentrating on the external context which will continue to determine the process of integration.

The key international determinant of the emergence of Community Europe was the threatening external environment at the height of the Cold War. Subsequent ossification of the Cold War was equally critical of the way in which the Community actually evolved. In one sense the immediate impact of the collapse of the Soviet Union and the end of the Cold War was simply to reinforce existing trends in integration. Reflex reactions to uncertainty are normally to hold on to what is left of the known. When, prior to the actual disintegration of the Soviet Union, it became clear that German reunification could be achieved on what could be considered the West's historic 'terms' – democracy and freedom for the new Germany to conduct its own foreign policy – immediate responses in much of Western Europe were reserved, even, in some cases, negative. The break-up of Yugoslavia and the consequent civil war seemed to demonstrate some of the advantages of the old certainties. For fifty years the standard response in Western Europe to any crisis had been to send or wait for the USA. However, with the removal of the Soviet threat, the USA has less motivation for involvement in European affairs. Failure of the European Union to recognise the implications of the resultant vacuum rested oddly with the Union's own ambitions in the fields of foreign affairs and security, as expressed at Maastricht.

The Yugoslav imbroglio both epitomises the new international scene and is an indication of the likely context of the international factors which now affect the Union. Disappearance of one of the super-powers suggests superficially a new world hegemony for the USA. The reality is different. Previously the USA could intervene world-wide both to block perceived Soviet threats and to safeguard a *status quo* ultimately supported by both super-powers. Within and outside the USA the climate was partial to the politics of intervention. These conditions have now disappeared. In reality, US domestic opinion had long since tired of policing the world and paying the cost. Throughout the Cold War it was easy enough for successive Presidents to play the anti-Communist card and equate interventionism with US national interest. This is no longer the case. Outside the USA perspectives have undergone an equivalent shift. The justification that the preservation of world stability requires US intervention has much less credibility now. This raises major issues for the Union.

To the East there is now an unstable power vacuum. Russia retains the potential to be a world power but there is no internal consensus on external aspirations. For over forty years Soviet-style Communism squeezed any independent political life and thought out of most of Eastern and Central Europe, and the consequences cannot be ignored.

Eastern Germany has in effect been absorbed into the Federal Republic, accepting most of the features of its political system and party families. Elsewhere in the former Soviet satellites the new political formations are of three kinds – vaguely reformist, strongly nationalist, or alternative vehicles for ex-Communists. It is hard to envisage these marrying easily with the party groupings which characterise the states of the Union. Quite apart from establishing stable political systems, the major problems confronting all the successor governments have been economic. The disappearance of the international economic structure and organisation which characterised the Soviet 'Empire' in Eastern and Central Europe has left another vacuum. Hasty attempts by Western entrepreneurs to step into the breach – and perhaps make large profits – have not helped promote economic stability.

The Union itself is a powerful pole of attraction, radiating relative stability and prosperity. In Central and Eastern Europe membership seems to offer some share in this stability and prosperity could be shared, whilst also offering an apparent guarantee against any return to the past. The Union's response is bound to be conditioned by a variety of factors. Back in the 1940s a major motivation for commencing the process of integration was the perceived need to find a stronger basis for Europe's relations with the external world, and above all to resolve the security threat endemic in a world in which the nexus of power had moved beyond the continent. The states and nations of Eastern and Central Europe are a reminder of that historic threat. At one level refusal, or even obstruction, of their entry is no more thinkable than it was with Greece, Portugal and Spain once they had established stable parliamentary democracies. On the other hand, few of the potential applicants in Central and Eastern Europe are anywhere near ready for either the political or economic implications of full membership. Their inclusion would impose a substantial economic burden on existing members. It would also inevitably transform the Union itself almost out of recognition. Certainly, the institutional structure, still bearing so many hallmarks of the original design for six, could not easily cope with four or five times that number of members. There may be little alternative: Europe is a small continent and the Union is bound to be affected by major events in neighbouring countries.

The impact on the Union of the transformation in the international system goes beyond the confines of the European continent. Russia is unlikely to replace the USSR as a world super-power, whilst the USA's reluctance to police every trouble spot extends beyond Europe. The major factors ensuring some kind of international stability have been removed. In so far as Europe's economic interests require political stability within many other regions, it may have to take a greater direct responsibility.

Sceptics have often contrasted the drive for regional unification with the increasingly integrated world economy. In reality there is no necessary incompatibility. Members of the European Union are all players in world-wide trade and capital markets. This global integration has been intensified by the communications and information technology revolution. Confronted with the sheer economic weight of the major players in this global market – especially Japan and the USA – individual European countries are at a clear disadvantage. Probably only Germany is in any position to compete as a player on its own. There is nothing new about any of this. Even in the 1950s it was one motivation for starting the process of European inegration. Later on, it was also the impact of these macro-economic factors which generated the first faltering steps by the Community into developing successively an external economic policy, political co-operation and EMS.

These are the external parameters which will condition the ongoing process of European integration. The future will resemble the past not because the external threats, dangers and challenges are the same: they have palpably changed and will continue to change. However, Europeans are still operating within a potentially hostile external context which is shaping a range of political, security and economic problems affecting the continent. It is hard to envisage a scenario in which these can be effectively managed without some kind of European entity. On this basis it is possible to argue that if the Community had never been created, the Union would still have to be invented.

The Union's internally generated agenda for the new IGC and beyond features six major issues – economic and monetary union, citizenship, justice and home affairs, foreign policy, institutional reform and enlargement. Whilst short-term solutions will reflect internal Union dynamics, the external context will ultimately be critical. Of all the subjects covered in the Treaty on European Union foreign and security policy demonstrates the greatest divergence between rhetoric and reality. Article J made the grandiloquent statement that 'a common foreign and security policy is hereby established'. However, neither within nor outside the Union is there any conception of what that means or what the policy contains other than a series of vague platitudes.

Supra-nationalists will claim that reliance on co-operation with a requirement for unanimity has been the major reason for the absence of significant progress since Maastricht. The most identifiable weakness has been lack of infrastructure. The Union has no independent capacity for analysis, preparation or planning: it is totally reliant on member state machinery. There is simply nothing to supply any institutional drive. It is unclear where responsibility lies for promoting agendas. Whilst successive Presidents can formulate goals for Community action during their six months in office, it is hard to see how this can apply in the same way to foreign and security issues. The Secretariat offers only a co-ordinating mechanism; the Commission is little more than an interested bystander.

The importance of external context for the future evolution of the second pillar of Maastricht is self-evident. There is widespread recognition of the need to strengthen the Union's external face. Arguments about procedures are rooted more in practicalities than fundamental principles. Whilst there is general recognition that at a formal level unanimity is likely to remain the norm, there is also some agreement on the need to find a basis for quick and flexible response by the Union to external events. The Union has to find means by which it can facilitate and implement policies in the European continent and also respond to crises.

There is a sense in which foreign policy comes of age when it acquires a security dimension. Throughout most of its history the Community was happy enough to ignore such issues. At a formal level NATO and the WEU were responsible. Neither the British nor the French independent nuclear deterrents altered the expectation that the USA would normally take the lead in security and defence issues affecting Europe. On the basis that integration is a process which will gradually lock together the governmental activity of the member states involved, it could be argued that ultimately the Community/Union would reach security as an area for some kind of joint activity. Such an approach is implied in the wording of the Single European Act, the first treaty to seek to include such issues under the collective umbrella: 'closer co-operation on questions of European security would contribute in an essential way to the development of a European identity in external policy matters'. However, in reality it has not been a question of the Community/Union reaching the security sector, but rather of security issues impacting on integration. In the context of the external world as it is in the mid-1990s the Union simply cannot ignore these issues.

Institutional debate within the Union is bound to focus on two issues. The first concerns the need for a single, over-arching and coherent decision-making structure which would apply to all three pillars of Maastricht. Given the inter-relationship of key issues – economic and monetary union, border controls, foreign policy and security – it is hard to envisage the Union being able to respond adequately to external challenge without a uniform institutional structure. The structure is also likely to have to cope with a larger membership than the present fifteen. The second issue is the nature of a single structure. The Community model is based on integration and supra-nationalism; that of the second and third Maastricht pillars on inter-governmental co-operation. This book cannot aspire to give any definitive answers, but there may be value in returning at the end of this concluding chapter to two of the ideas introduced in Chapter 1. The first concerns the German problem. The Federal Republic found a niche within the old, pre 1989 Europe: a model of political stability, an apparently permanently buoyant economy, a key prop of all Western organisations. The balancing factor was that the external context ensured strict limitations on Germany's political power. In the new Europe the balancing factors have been removed and reunited Germany has the potential to dominate Europe and the Union. Any reversion to the old-fashioned state system would make it far easier for that potential to be realised. The notion of European integration as a mechanism for containment of Germany has, if anything, been reinforced. This view is certainly one of the major reasons for undiminished French enthusiasm for EMU. The Deutschmark is Europe's strongest currency. In the absence of monetary union, it will become Europe's dominant currency. EMU offers an institutional structure for some European political control.

The second idea relates to the concept of federalism – the dreaded 'F' word in British politics. Europe will be integrated in that almost all countries will be members of a single major organisation dedicated to collective decision over a vast swathe of governmental activity. Whilst national diversity will remain, there will be a parallel European identity – part of the world polity. Integration will be conducted through a continuum of procedures, ranging from the purely inter-governmental through to the supra-national model. For most global purposes Europe will be a single entity.

In the first chapter I attempted a definition of federalism in a European context:-'*a new and complete constitution for Europe with a specific transfer of powers to the new "supra-national" institutions. The basic characteristic of federalism lies in the existence of two tiers of government – one for the entire federation and one for its constituent parts (in this case the member countries). Powers are distributed between the two tiers by a written constitution or treaty. Each tier is fully autonomous and neither can remove, or interfere with the powers of, the other. Each will have an independent source of revenue with which to fulfil its role'.*

Few concepts have been as much misunderstood as federalism. The above definition makes it clear that federalism is not an absolute. There are many different models and types of federal states and this is because federalism is itself a continuum and most of its characteristics are relative. The European Union is never going to be a centralised state, but it is already far more than a simple international organisation. Over the years its federal characteristics have gradually increased. Decisions to be made in the forthcoming years will confirm the process. It is always possible to use such terms as quasi- or neo-federalism. Of course this does differentiate between the European Union and more established or complete federations such as Switzerland or the USA. Perhaps, though, this has become no more than a semantic game. To all intents and purposes Britain is now part of a federal Europe.

Notes

1 EUROPE IN 1945

1 See R.J. Crampton, *Eastern Europe in the Twentieth Century*, Routledge, 1994. For the purpose of the analysis in these paragraphs I am, slightly arbitrarily, including Austria as part of Central and Eastern Europe. It was, after all, technically a successor state.

2 Whilst Finland and Yugoslavia were clearly within the Soviet sphere of influence neither was in the Soviet bloc as such. Finland was 'allowed' to be a parliamentary democracy – in effect so long as she preserved her neutrality and did not involve herself in 'anti-Soviet' actions. Russian armies had played little role in the liberation of Yugoslavia and Tito was strong enough to maintain an independent Communist regime beyond Soviet control.

3 See *Documents on British Policy Overseas*, series 2 ,vol. 1, pp. 812–13.

4 Quoted in H. Luethy, *France against Herself*, Praeger, 1955.

5 Cited by Luethy, ibid. Evidently from an article in *Année Politique et Economique* (1953) visualising nation states as embodying progress beyond the one Europe!

6 Alan Milward, *The European Rescue of the Nation State*, Routledge, 1992.

7 For an extremely detailed account of the early development of the European Movement, see Walter Lipgens, *A History of European Integration 1945–7*, Clarendon Press, 1982.

2 THE CONTEXT FOR INTEGRATION

1 The two most important books are: Ernst Haas, *The Uniting of Europe*, Stevens, 1958; and Leon Lindberg,*The Political Dynamics of European Economic Integration*, Stanford, 1963.

2 Technically there are three European communities, based on three separate treaties. It has long been custom and practice to refer to the European Economic Community as the European Community and this has now been made official by the Maastricht Treaty. In general usage the term 'European Community', or just 'Community', simply absorbs the other two communities. See also Glossary of Main Terms.

3 The flavour of the difference between these two 'European' 'isms' may be savoured through the writings of Altiero Spinelli (federalist) and David Mitrany (functionalist). Reference to writings by their modern 'disciples' may be instructive: see M. Burgess, *Federalism and European Union*, Routledge, 1989; and Paul Taylor, *The Limits of European Integration*, Croom Helm, 1983.

4 A process described in, and evocatively suggested in the very title of, Alan Milward, *The European Rescue of the Nation-State*, Routledge, 1992.

5 See Haas, *The Uniting of Europe*.

6 This phrase was frequently used by President de Gaulle as his vision of Europe.

7 All three are established parliamentary democracies. Austrian neutrality had been a condition for Soviet agreement to end allied occupation. Finland, as an immediate neighbour of the Soviet Union, had to direct its foreign policy accordingly. Sweden had opted quite freely for a policy of neutrality between the super-powers.

8 A phrase much in vogue within the Community which refers to the 'whole range of principles, policies, laws, practices, obligations and objectives which have been agreed ... including the Treaties in their entirety'; see T.Bainbridge and A. Teasdale, *The Penguin Companion to European Union*, Penguin, 1995.

3 THE EMERGENCE OF THE SIX

1 H. Luethy, *France against Herself*, Praeger, 1955.

2 Inclusion of Finland within 'Western Europe' shows the difficulty of categorisation. Geographically, it is well to the east of the continent. Militarily, it was neutral. It was, however, a stable parliamentary democracy, although like France and Italy it possessed a large Communist Party. (See also note 2 to Chapter 1.)

3 Luethy, *France against Herself*.

4 Jean Monnet is usually considered to be the 'father' of European integration. See Jean Monnet, *Memoirs*, Collins, 1978; and François Duchêne, *Jean Monnet: the First Statesman of Interdependence*, Norton, 1994.

5 A Conservative government replaced Labour in October 1951. Despite Prime Minister Churchill's well-known pro-European rhetoric, it made no discernible difference to attitudes towards integration.

6 In retrospect, a clear justification for publication of Jean Monnet's *Les Etats-Unis d'Europe ont Commencé*, Laffont; Paris, 1955. The title in English is 'The United States of Europe has begun'.

7 See Roy Pryce (ed.), *The Dynamics of European Union*, Croom Helm, 1987. It was during these negotiations that various delegations proposed that the ultimate aim should be a common market.

8 See Paul-Henri Spaak, *The Continuing Battle: Memoirs of a European 1936–66*, Weidenfeld and Nicolson, 1971. Spaak makes it clear that he did not write the report which bears his name. The principal author was Pierre Uri, who had been recommended to Spaak by Jean Monnet.

9 The best account is M. Camps, *Britain and the European Community 1955–63*, Oxford University Press, 1965.

10 Ratification was approved in the National Assembly with 342 votes in favour and 239 against. This compares with a vote of 376 against 240 to ratify the ECSC. Ratification of the EDC was lost on a technical vote by 319 against 264. See F.R. Willis, *France, Germany and the New Europe*, Oxford University Press, 2nd edn, 1965.

4 THE EUROPEAN COMMUNITY

1 See Chapter 8.
2 See *Treaties Establishing the European Communities*, Publications Office of the European Communities, Luxembourg. Also *European Community Treaties*, Sweet and Maxwell. In each case there are various editions.
3 See Chapter 3.
4 See Chapter 3.
5 See Chapter 8 for changes introduced by the Maastricht Treaty.
6 The term is French and does not have the same connotation as the same word in English. The nearest equivalent to the French cabinet is the ministerial private office.
7 See note 8 to Chapter 2.
8 See Chapters 6 and 8.
9 Britain, Denmark and Ireland joined on 1 January 1973, Greece on 1 January 1981, Portugal and Spain on 1 January 1986, Austria, Finland and Sweden on 1 January 1995.
10 Expenditure was divided into two categories – obligatory and non-obligatory. Obligatory expenditure was that incurred as a direct result of the original treaties. Broadly speaking, both Parliament and the Council are required to vote the budget. However, in the event of dispute Council has the final word on obligatory expenditure (which includes the cost of the CAP) and Parliament on non-obligatory expenditure.
11 See chapter by N. March-Hunnings on the Court of Justice in S. Henig, *Power and Decision in Europe*, Europotentials Press, 1980.

5 THE SIX IN SEARCH OF AN IDENTITY

1 The government of Mendès-France which took office in 1954 was the most effective in the life of the Fourth Republic. Mendès-France earned the undying hostility of the pro-European MRP as a result of his refusal to support the EDC, and ultimately this helped precipitate his downfall. Few governments of the Fourth Republic before or after that of Mendès-France possessed credibility or authority. His government was able to resolve outstanding imperial issues in both Indo-China in Morocco/Tunisia. No subsequent government was able to tackle the Algerian problem with any success.
2 For a recent and highly readable history of the Fourth Republic, see F. Giles, *The Locust Years: the Story of the French Fourth Republic, 1946–58*, Secker and Warburg, 1991.
3 An unpublished manuscript by Edmond Jouve of the Faculty de Droit et des Sciences Sociales, University of Paris, entitled 'Le Thème Européen

dans les écrits et les déclarations du Général de Gaulle' is an invaluable source. As early as July 1952 de Gaulle asserted, 'we cannot construct Europe without its peoples'. And at a press conference in September 1960 – 'To build, that is to unite Europe is essential . . . but it is necessary to base this on realities not on dreams . . . . The European realities . . . are the states' (my translation).

4 'Of course we can establish particular structures which are more or less extra-national. These structures have some technical value, but they do not, and cannot, have any authority and in consequence cannot be politically effective.' See Jouve, ibid.

5 An interesting 'tract for the times' written by a staunch federalist gives the flavour of this approach: 'Monnet's Europe . . . is liberal, democratic, humane . . . de Gaulle's . . . .is authoritarian, chauvinist . . . and likely . . . to undermine the West's ability to help solve the vast and terrible problems that confront the world.' John Pinder, *Europe against de Gaulle*, Pall Mall, 1963.

6 Austria, Britain, Denmark, Norway, Portugal, Sweden and Switzerland.

7 See M. Camps, *Britain and the European Community 1955–63*, Oxford University Press, 1965.

8 For a good account of the negotiations see R. Pryce (ed.), *The Dynamics of European Union*, Croom Helm, 1987.

9 For a detailed account see J. Newhouse, *Collision in Brussels: the Common Market Crisis of 30 June 1965*, Faber, 1967. It makes heavy reading, but the author deserves acknowledgement as being one of the first to recognise that 'The Common Market is too little thought of in a broad political context and too much regarded as an instrument that will grow and flourish, or decline and wither on its own merits.'

10 For further analysis see S. Henig, *Power and Decision in Europe*, Europotentials Press, 1980.

11 See Chapter 8.

6 WIDENING AND DEEPENING

1 'Spill-over' was a concept much in vogue in the early years of the Community, particularly amongst some academic observers. The theory was that each common policy would itself generate needs for other policies. Internal Community dynamics would thus lead to a semi-automatic extension of the scope of integration. Thus implementation of the customs union was the reason for initial of social and regional policies.

2 See D. Dinan, *Ever Closer Union*, Macmillan, 1994; and R. Pryce (ed.), *The Dynamics of European Union*, Croom Helm, 1987.

3 For further details see D. Dinan, *Ever Closer Union*; T. Bainbridge and A. Teasdale, *The Penguin Companion to European Union*, Penguin, 1995; and M. Shackleton, *Financing the European Union*, 1990.

4 See note 8 to Chapter 2 and also Glossary of Major Terms and Abbreviations.

5 For a full account of the development of the new machinery see Simon Nuttall, *European Political Co-operation*, Oxford University Press, 1992.

6 See Mary Johnston, *The European Council: Gatekeeper of the European Community*, Westview, 1994.

7 Not surprisingly, European elections have spawned a whole crop of literature of their own. Examples are J. Lodge, *The 1989 Election of the European Parliament*, Macmillan, 1990; and D. Butler and M. Westlake, *British Politics and European Elections*, Macmillan, 1995.

8 See S. Henig, *Power and Decision in Europe*, Europotentials Press, 1980, for a fuller discussion of reports by Vedel, Spierenburg and the 'Committee of Three'.

9 See Roy Jenkins, *European Diary 1977–81*, Collins, 1989.

10 For a full explanation of EMS as well as the exchange rate mechanism, etc., see D. Swann, *The Economics of the Common Market* (8th edn), Penguin, 1995.

11 See Chapters 8 and 9.

12 Swann, *The Economics of the Common Market*.

7 FROM COMMUNITY TO UNION

1 The British budgetary problem was based on the juxtaposition of two factors. The nature of the 'own resources' of the Community meant that for technical reasons Britain would make an excessive gross contribution. Since the largest part of the budget was spent on agriculture, Britain also received disproportionately little back. As a result it was a major net contributor, way out of proportion to both its size and wealth.

2 Hans Dietrich Genscher, a leading member of the German Free Democratic Party, was Foreign Minister of the Federal Republic from 1974 until 1992. The Free Democrats were junior partners in successive coalitions with the larger Social Democrats and Christian Democrats. Genscher was largely reponsible for the change in government in 1982 when Kohl became Chancellor.

3 See T. Bainbridge and A. Teasdale, *The Penguin Companion to European Union*, 1995, and R. Pryce, *The Dynamics of European Union*, Croom Helm, 1987.

4 Altiero Spinelli enjoyed a long and unique career as an active federalist, a Commissioner and subsequently a Member of the European Parliament. See also Chapter 2 and M. Burgess, *Federalism and European Union*, Routledge, 1989.

5 See Pryce, *The Dynamics of European Union*.

6 The VAT maximum was increased from 1 to 1.4%. Later in the decade this too would prove inadequate and an extra resource – a national levy based on GNP – was introduced.

7 The point is made in Bainbridge and Teasdale, *The Penguin Companion to European Union*, Burgess, *Federalism and European Union*, and Pryce, *The Dynamics of European Union*.

8 E Haas, *The Uniting of Europe*, Stevens, 1958.

9 See in particular Dinan, *Ever Closer Union*, Macmillan, 1994.

10 See Chapter 9.

8 MAASTRICHT AND EUROPEAN UNION

1 There were major reports in the 1970s by Vedal, Tindemanns, Spierenburg and the Committee of Three. These were followed in the 1980s by the Genscher-Colombo plan, Parliament's draft Treaty of European Union and the Dooge report. For actual documents, see *Selection of Texts concerning Institutional Matters of the Community 1950–82*, European Parliament. For academic discussion see S. Henig, *Power and Decision in Europe*, Europotentials Press, 1980; R. Pryce (ed.), *The Dynamics of European Union*; and M. Burgess, *Federalism and European Union*, Routledge, 1989.

2 See Henig, *Power and Decision in Europe*.

3 See Chapter 5.

4 At the Paris conference in October 1972 the Head of Government of the Six and the three new members agreed on 'the major objective of transforming before the end of the decade ... the whole complex of the relations of Member States into a European Union'. In the absence of any substantive progress the commitment was reaffirmed (more than a decade later and with a different time span!) by the Solemn Declaration of Stuttgart in June 1983.

5 The term 'European Community' is used for the first time in a treaty text. Formally the European Economic Community is renamed the European Community.

6 A. Duff (ed.), *Maastricht and Beyond: Building the European Union*, for Federal Trust, Routledge, 1994.

7 Although the word is not used in the treaty, this procedure is correctly described as 'co-decision' since legislation cannot take effect without the agreement of both Parliament and Council. It is interesting to compare legislative with budgetary procedures. The co-operation procedure introduced by the Single European Act is essentially the same as that which applies to obligatory expenditure. Parliament participates fully in the decision-making process but Council has the final say. However, the 'co-decision procedure' introduced by the Treaty on European Union is different from that which applies to non-obligatory expenditure. For non-obligatory expenditure Parliament has the final say. Under co-decision, Parliament and Council are equal. All this and much else is discussed and dissected in C. Church and D. Phinnemore, *European Union and European Community: a Handbook and Commentary on the Post-Maastricht treaties*, Harvester Wheatsheaf, 1994.

8 This implies five types of Parliamentary activity in the decision-making process. In fact, the ways in which other institutions exercise their constitutional powers also vary. In all there are in excess of twenty different decision-making procedures for the Community pillar.

9 Of the twelve members at the time of signing the Maastricht Treaty only Ireland was neutral. The subsequent enlargement involved three countries – Austria, Finland and Sweden – all of which had been neutral in defence issues. Of the fifteen member states, eleven are in NATO and two of those (France and Greece) are not part of the joint military command. Originally the WEU consisted of the first six members of the Community plus Britain (see Chapter 3). Subsequently Greece, Portugal

and Spain have joined, whilst the other Union members (including the neutrals) have observer status.

10 As it happens, the period in question involved considerable joint activity in the defence sphere, largely as a result of the civil war in former Yugoslavia. However the European instrument for this was the WEU.

Glossary of major terms and abbreviations

'ACQUIS COMMUNAUTAIRE' = the sum of all Community treaties and policies to date. It became an article of faith for the original members, for the Commission and for most proponents of European integration that potential new members would be required to accept the 'acquis' in its entirety as a prelude to entry.

COMMISSION = appointed executive and administrative authority of European Community. Although members of the Commission are appointed by member states and all are represented, they have to take an oath not to accept instructions from national governments.

COMMITTEE OF PERMANENT REPRESENTATIVES (COREPER) = committee of national government ambassadors to the European Community which meets weekly to plan the work of the Council of Ministers.

COMMON AGRICULTURAL POLICY (CAP) = system for fixing prices and guaranteeing farming income inside the European Community. There is a guaranteed price for production up to a certain level, whilst customs duties are imposed on many food imports. Expenditure is incurred on both the guaranteed prices and on structural funds to help in the rationalisation and modernisation of the agricultural industry.

COMMON MARKET = key objective of the European Economic Community (see below). Implies removal of all internal tariffs and other trade barriers, but with a common external tariff applying to imports from other countries.

COMMUNITY = shortened term for European Community.

COMMUNITY METHOD = slightly vague term used by proponents of the Community as an idealised description of a way of 'doing business'. In essence, it subordinates discussion of details to commitments on principle. Once the member states have determined the principles and, therefore, reached 'agreements to agree', the institutions will sort out the details.

COUNCIL OF MINISTERS = rule-making body with major legislative power in European Community. Includes ministers from all member states. Most decisions can be taken by a system of qualified majority voting.

COURT OF JUSTICE = supreme legal body within the Community. Interprets treaties and subsequent Community legislation. Determines disputes on Community issues between institutions and member states.

ECONOMIC AND MONETARY UNION (EMU) = co-ordination and harmonisation of economic and monetary policy of member states of Community leading to an integrated European economy with a single European currency.

ECU = notional currency used for all transactions inside European Community. Established 1981. Its value is determined by reference to a weighted 'basket' of national currencies. Will be the unit for the single currency.

ENLARGEMENT = admission of new members. After earlier abortive negotiations, Britain, Denmark and Ireland joined in 1973; Greece in 1981; Portugal and Spain in 1986; Austria, Finland and Sweden in 1995. Only European democracies are eligible.

EURATOM = one of the three originally separate communities established by the Six through the Treaty of Rome. Aim to pool nuclear research technology.

EUROPEAN COAL AND STEEL COMMUNITY (ECSC) = first of the three communities established by the Six through the Treaty of Paris. Aim of joint management of coal and steel industries. Based on the Schuman plan, named after the French Foreign Minister, it started the process of integration.

EUROPEAN COMMUNITY (EC) = joint term for the three communities. Sometimes abbreviated to Community. The term was given legal force by the Maastricht Treaty on European Union.

EUROPEAN COUNCIL = forum for heads of government of member states of European Community. Gives broad direction to all joint activities. Introduced in the 1970s but not given legal force until the Single European Act.

EUROPEAN DEFENCE COMMUNITY (EDC) = abortive attempt in the 1950s by the Six to integrate defence policies and establish a European army.

EUROPEAN ECONOMIC COMMUNITY = most important of three communities established by the Six through the Treaty of Rome. Aim to establish a customs union and to develop joint economic policies, e.g., for agriculture, competition, etc.

EUROPEAN MONETARY SYSTEM (EMS) = system for supporting national currencies and, through what is known as the exchange rate mechanism, for preventing exchange fluctuations – established 1981.

EUROPEAN PARLIAMENT = parliamentary assembly of European Community. Initially made up of representatives from national parliaments, it has since 1979 directly elected at five-yearly intervals. Its powers are much more limited than those of national parliaments.

EUROPEAN POLITICAL CO-OPERATION (EPC) = system established in 1970 to bring about co-operation on issues of foreign policy. Given legal foundation by the Single European Act.

EUROPEAN UNION = aim of bringing together all activities linking member countries of the Community. Concept developed in 1970s under a single structure. The Maastricht Treaty represented the first formal steps towards implementation.

FEDERALISM = formal splitting of governmental powers between (normally) two different tiers or levels of authority. Based on law or treaty. Germany, Switzerland and USA all have federal systems of government. Whilst the actual distribution of powers varies, each tier must have an independent source of revenue. Constitutional amendment requires the agreement of both tiers.

FUNCTIONALISM = often seen as an alternative to federalism. Countries agree on establishing supra-national institutions with powers over particular sectors of governmental activity.

HIGH AUTHORITY = executive and administrative authority of European Coal and Steel Community. After 1967 absorbed into Commission.

INTEGRATION = concept of merging activities of different countries in particular spheres of activity. Involves establishing joint procedures. Basic principle underpinning European Community. Assumed that the scope of integration will gradually expand to cover an increasing range of governmental and other activities.

INTER-GOVERNMENTAL CONFERENCE (IGC) = meeting of representatives of governments of member states of the Community/Union outside the regular institutions to develop major initiatives, particularly new treaties. This was the mechanism used to prepare for and negotiate both the Single European Act and the Maastricht Treaty on European Union.

IRON CURTAIN = dividing line between Eastern and Western Europe after Second World War with former under Soviet influence/control. Disappeared between 1989 and 1991.

LUXEMBOURG COMPROMISE = name given to agreements which ended the Community crisis in the mid 1960s. In reality it is a misnomer, since the key issue was the question of majority voting and the six then members only agreed to differ.

MAASTRICHT TREATY = Treaty on European Union signed in 1991 and implemented in 1993. Formally committed Community members to a range of new activities, particularly Economic and Monetary Union, co-operation in Justice and Home Affairs and the establishment of a common foreign and security policy.

OWN RESOURCES = Community revenue for financing expenditure. Established by 1970 and 1975 treaties. The proceeds of the common external tariff and levies on agricultural imports together with a uniform rate of VAT 'belong' to the Community. Subsequently the Community has been given another resource – in effect, national contributions based on GNP.

SINGLE EUROPEAN ACT (SEA) = 1986 treaty committing Community members to a single market. Also gave legal basis to European Council and European Political Co-operation.

SINGLE MARKET = removal of all barriers and obstacles to trade. The Common Market removed tariff barriers. The Single Europan Act committed member states to a detailed programme for establishing a single market by the end of 1992.

(THE) SIX = founder members of the three communities (ECSC, EEC and Euratom – see above). They were Belgium, France, Germany, Italy, Luxembourg and the Netherlands.

SUBSIDIARITY = principle of taking decisions and making policy at lowest possible level. Introduced into the Maastricht Treaty on British insistence. The principle only applies to national as against European action and has no bearing on national approaches to decision taking at regional and local level.

SUPRA-NATIONALISM = action above the level of nation states; hence supra-national institutions operate over and above national governments, etc. This approach is a cornerstone of the Community.

TREATY OF PARIS = treaty establishing the European Coal and Steel Community, signed in 1951.

TREATY OF ROME = normally treaty establishing the European Economic Community signed in 1957. There were actually two treaties signed at Rome – the other established Euratom.

VETO = idea that decisions can only be taken by unanimity. Hence any one country has the right to veto. Whilst de Gaulle was President, the veto was a key part of French Community policy. Subsequently Britain has been the main champion. Most member countries feel it should be reserved for constitutional issues, new treaty commitments and the adhesion of new members.

WESTERN EUROPEAN UNION = treaty signed in 1955 between Britain, France, Germany, Italy and the Benelux countries. Building on the 1948 Treaty between Britain, France and the Benelux, it facilitated, and laid down controls on, German rearmament, and committed Britain to keep armed forces on the European mainland.

An annotated selective bibliography

There is now a vast literature on all aspects of European integration, but it is worth bearing in mind that the Community/Union has been in continuous evolution so that much of this earlier material has become dated. A complete bibliography would be well beyond the scope of this volume. I have simply listed with very brief comments those books which may be particularly interesting and useful for those who have not hitherto specialised in the field.

Arter, D. *The Politics of European Integration in the Twentieth Century*, Dartmouth, 1993, p. 309.
Broad historic approach, placing integration in context of European history since 1919.

Bainbridge, T. with Teasdale, A. *The Penguin Companion to European Union*, Penguin, 1995, p. 502.
Presented as a dictionary; well-researched and comprehensive. This really is an outstanding work and it is essential for students!

Church, C. and Phinnemore, D. *European Union and European Community*, Harvester Wheatsheaf, 1994, p. 575.
Sub-titled 'A Handbook and Commentary on the Post-Maastricht Treaties', it reprints the texts with authoritative commentary.

Corbett, R., Jacobs, F. and Shackleton, M. *The European Parliament*, (3rd edn), Cartermill, 1995, p. 357.
The authors are all insiders and this is now the established classic text on the Parliament.

Dinan, D. *Ever Closer Union: an Introduction to the European Community*, Macmillan, 1994, p. 553.
A highly readable account of the development, institutions and policies of the Community.

Duff, A. Pinder, J. and Pryce, R. (eds for the Federal Trust), *Maastricht and Beyond*, Routledge,1994, p. 311.

Sub-titled 'Building the European Union', this collective work assesses Maastricht and looks to future developments.

Edwards, G. and Spence, D. (eds), *The European Commission*, Longman, 1994, p. 311.
Another collective work, this is a comprehensive and very detailed examination of the work of the Commission.

D. Gowland, D., O'Neill, B. and Reid, A., *The European Mosaic: Contemporary Politics, Economics and Culture*, Longman, 1995, p. 329.
Introduction to cross-disciplinary study offering basis for assessing what is Europe and who are the Europeans.

Hayes-Renshaw, F. and Wallace, H., *The Council of Ministers*, Macmillan, 1997, p. 340.
Comprehensive and detailed survey of what is really the most powerful Community institution.

Nelsen, B. and Stubb, A., *The European Union: Readings of the Theory and Practice of European Integration*, Rienner, 1994, p. 307.
Useful collection of basic statements by activists and articles by academics (distributed outside USA by Macmillan).

Nicoll, W. and Salmon, T., *Understanding the New European Community*, Harvester Wheatsheaf, 1994, p. 350.
Authors are a partnership of practitioner and academic. Well-presented, insightful survey of how the Community works and what it does.

Nugent, N., *Government and Politics of the European Union*, Macmillan, 1994, p. 473.
Established as the core textbook on the politics of the Community/Union, its operation and key policy sectors.

Nuttall, S., *European Political Co-operation*,Oxford University Press, 1992, p. 342.
Another 'insider' book, tracing the development and structure of political co-operation pre-Maastricht.

O'Neill, M, *The Politics of European Integration: a Reader*, Routledge, 1996, p. 343.
Excellent, but advanced symposium.

Richardson, J. (ed.), *European Union: Power and Policy-Making*, Routledge, 1996, p. 300.
Another very fine symposium dealing with perhaps the key issue in understanding the Community/Union.

Swann, D., *The Economics of the Common Market: Integration in the European Union* (8th edn), Penguin, 1995, p. 405.

First published in 1970 and a permanent feature amongst the basic texts. Accessible to the non-specialist.

Wallace, H. and Wallace, W., *Policy Making in the European Union*, Oxford University Press, 1996, p. 509.
Major, advanced study of how policies are made in the Community/Union, with documented and detailed case studies.

Welsh, M., *Europe United?*, Macmillan, 1996, p. 196.

Valuable introduction, particularly for students, to Maastricht and the Union, by a former MEP.

Westlake, M., *The Council of the European Union*, Cartermill, 1995, p. 415.

Massive and complex work, written from the inside, on the Council in all its manifestations, with many tables, charts, etc.

Index